Think About Reading

3

Logic-Based Reading Series

WorldCom Edu

Table of **Contents**

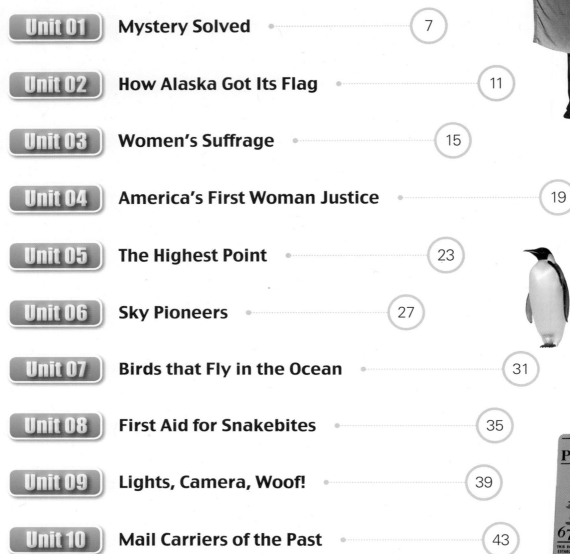

Unit 01	**Mystery Solved**	7
Unit 02	**How Alaska Got Its Flag**	11
Unit 03	**Women's Suffrage**	15
Unit 04	**America's First Woman Justice**	19
Unit 05	**The Highest Point**	23
Unit 06	**Sky Pioneers**	27
Unit 07	**Birds that Fly in the Ocean**	31
Unit 08	**First Aid for Snakebites**	35
Unit 09	**Lights, Camera, Woof!**	39
Unit 10	**Mail Carriers of the Past**	43

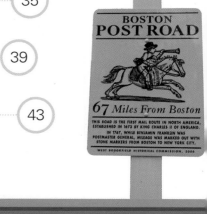

BOSTON
POST ROAD

67 Miles From Boston

THIS ROAD IS THE FIRST MAIL ROUTE IN NORTH AMERICA,
ESTABLISHED IN 1673 BY KING CHARLES II OF ENGLAND.
IN 1767, WHILE BENJAMIN FRANKLIN WAS
POSTMASTER GENERAL, MILEAGE WAS MARKED OUT WITH
STONE MARKERS FROM BOSTON TO NEW YORK CITY.

WEST BROOKFIELD HISTORICAL COMMISSION, 2006

Unit 11 Nantucket Sleighride 47

Unit 12 Forgotten Inventions 51

Unit 13 Bat Talk! 55

Unit 14 An Island Rises from the Sea 59

Unit 15 Small but Noisy 63

Unit 16 The Dancing Stallions 67

Unit 17 Deep-Sea Adventure 71

Unit 18 A Dog's Best Friend 75

Unit 19 Mounties, Past and Present 79

Unit 20 No Strings or Wings 83

Features

The *Thinking About Reading* series are aimed at helping students to master key reading skills as well as logical thinking skills.

Thinking Aloud and Words in Passage

- Presents attractive images associated with reading passages

- Allows the reader to familiarize key vocabulary words in the reading passage

Reading

- Covers various content areas such as science and social studies

- Provides highly engaging and relevant content for teenage readers

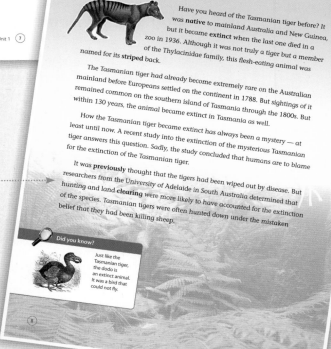

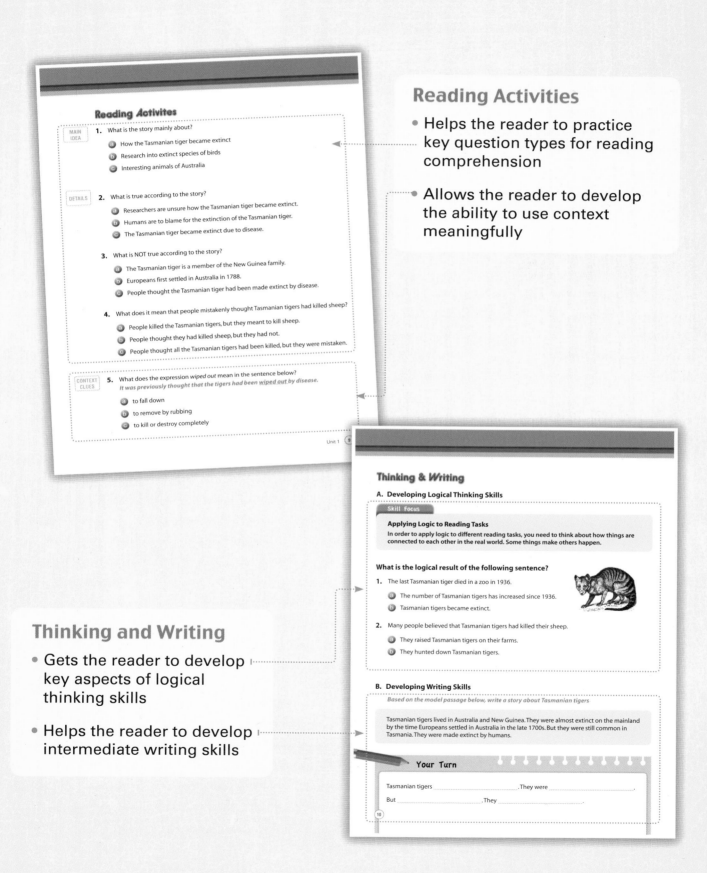

Reading Activites

MAIN IDEA
1. What is the story mainly about?
   a. How the Tasmanian tiger became extinct
   b. Research into extinct species of birds
   c. Interesting animals of Australia

DETAILS
2. What is true according to the story?
   a. Researchers are unsure how the Tasmanian tiger became extinct.
   b. Humans are to blame for the extinction of the Tasmanian tiger.
   c. The Tasmanian tiger became extinct due to disease.

3. What is NOT true according to the story?
   a. The Tasmanian tiger is a member of the New Guinea family.
   b. Europeans first settled in Australia in 1788.
   c. People thought the Tasmanian tiger had been made extinct by disease.

4. What does it mean that people mistakenly thought Tasmanian tigers had killed sheep?
   a. People killed the Tasmanian tigers, but they meant to kill sheep.
   b. People thought they had killed sheep, but they had not.
   c. People thought all the Tasmanian tigers had been killed, but they were mistaken.

CONTEXT CLUES
5. What does the expression *wiped out* mean in the sentence below?
   It was previously thought that the tigers had been <u>wiped out</u> by disease.
   a. to fall down
   b. to remove by rubbing
   c. to kill or destroy completely

Unit 1 9

Reading Activities

- Helps the reader to practice key question types for reading comprehension

- Allows the reader to develop the ability to use context meaningfully

Thinking & Writing

A. Developing Logical Thinking Skills

Skill Focus

Applying Logic to Reading Tasks
In order to apply logic to different reading tasks, you need to think about how things are connected to each other in the real world. Some things make others happen.

What is the logical result of the following sentence?

1. The last Tasmanian tiger died in a zoo in 1936.
   a. The number of Tasmanian tigers has increased since 1936.
   b. Tasmanian tigers became extinct.

2. Many people believed that Tasmanian tigers had killed their sheep.
   a. They raised Tasmanian tigers on their farms.
   b. They hunted down Tasmanian tigers.

B. Developing Writing Skills

Based on the model passage below, write a story about Tasmanian tigers

Tasmanian tigers lived in Australia and New Guinea. They were almost extinct on the mainland by the time Europeans settled in Australia in the late 1700s. But they were still common in Tasmania. They were made extinct by humans.

Your Turn

Tasmanian tigers _____. They were _____
But _____. They _____

10

Thinking and Writing

- Gets the reader to develop key aspects of logical thinking skills

- Helps the reader to develop intermediate writing skills

Mystery Solved

1 Tasmanian Tiger

Thinking Aloud

Look at the picture above and answer the following questions.

1. Do you know what this animal is?
2. It has been extinct for many years. Can you name some other extinct animals?

Words in Passage

Match the word with its definition.

_____ **1.** native   ⓐ to remove things from a place

_____ **2.** striped   ⓑ not existing anymore

_____ **3.** previously   ⓒ living in a particular place

_____ **4.** extinct   ⓓ having lines of color

_____ **5.** clear   ⓔ before now

Mystery Solved

Have you heard of the Tasmanian tiger before? It was **native** to mainland Australia and New Guinea, but it became **extinct** when the last one died in a zoo in 1936. Although it was not truly a tiger but a member of the Thylacinidae family, this flesh-eating animal was named for its **striped** back.

The Tasmanian tiger had already become extremely rare on the Australian mainland before Europeans settled on the continent in 1788. But sightings of it remained common on the southern island of Tasmania through the 1800s. But within 130 years, the animal became extinct in Tasmania as well.

How the Tasmanian tiger became extinct has always been a mystery — at least until now. A recent study into the extinction of the mysterious Tasmanian tiger answers this question. Sadly, the study concluded that humans are to blame for the extinction of the Tasmanian tiger.

It was **previously** thought that the tigers had been wiped out by disease. But researchers from the University of Adelaide in South Australia determined that hunting and land **clearing** were more likely to have accounted for the extinction of the species. Tasmanian tigers were often hunted down under the mistaken belief that they had been killing sheep.

Did you know?

Just like the Tasmanian tiger, the dodo is an extinct animal. It was a bird that could not fly.

Reading Activites

MAIN IDEA

1. What is the story mainly about?

- **a** How the Tasmanian tiger became extinct
- **b** Research into extinct species of birds
- **c** Interesting animals of Australia

DETAILS

2. What is true according to the story?

- **a** Researchers are unsure how the Tasmanian tiger became extinct.
- **b** Humans are to blame for the extinction of the Tasmanian tiger.
- **c** The Tasmanian tiger became extinct due to disease.

3. What is NOT true according to the story?

- **a** The Tasmanian tiger is a member of the New Guinea family.
- **b** Europeans first settled in Australia in 1788.
- **c** People thought the Tasmanian tiger had been made extinct by disease.

4. What does it mean that people mistakenly thought Tasmanian tigers had killed sheep?

- **a** People killed the Tasmanian tigers, but they meant to kill sheep.
- **b** People thought they had killed sheep, but they had not.
- **c** People thought all the Tasmanian tigers had been killed, but they were mistaken.

CONTEXT CLUES

5. What does the expression *wiped out* mean in the sentence below?
It was previously thought that the tigers had been <u>wiped out</u> by disease.

- **a** to fall down
- **b** to remove by rubbing
- **c** to kill or destroy completely

Thinking & Writing

A. Developing Logical Thinking Skills

Skill Focus

Applying Logic to Reading Tasks

In order to apply logic to different reading tasks, you need to think about how things are connected to each other in the real world. Some things make others happen.

What is the logical result of the following sentence?

1. The last Tasmanian tiger died in a zoo in 1936.

    a The number of Tasmanian tigers has increased since 1936.

    b Tasmanian tigers became extinct.

2. Many people believed that Tasmanian tigers had killed their sheep.

    a They raised Tasmanian tigers on their farms.

    b They hunted down Tasmanian tigers.

B. Developing Writing Skills

Based on the model passage below, write a story about Tasmanian tigers.

Tasmanian tigers lived in Australia and New Guinea. They were almost extinct on the mainland by the time Europeans settled in Australia in the late 1700s. But they were still common in Tasmania. They were made extinct by humans.

Your Turn

Tasmanian tigers _____. They were _____.

But _____. They _____.

Unit 02

How Alaska Got Its Flag

ALASKA

Thinking Aloud

Look at the picture above and answer the following questions.

1. Do you know which American state this flag belongs to?
2. What do you think the parts of the flag represent?

Words in Passage

Match the word with its definition.

_____ **1.** governor

_____ **2.** territory

_____ **3.** state

_____ **4.** upbringing

_____ **5.** symbolize

ⓐ to stand for something

ⓑ a political unit that can be found in the US

ⓒ the way in which a child is raised

ⓓ the leader of a state or territory

ⓔ land that is controlled by a certain country

How Alaska Got Its Flag

Before 1927, Alaska did not have a flag, and it was still just a **territory**. In 1926, Alaska's **governor** thought having a flag would help Alaska become a **state**.

To find a unique flag, a contest was held among Alaskan schoolchildren. The winning design was to be used in planning Alaska's flag.

The winner of the design contest was a 13-year-old boy named Benny Benson. Benny lived in an orphanage in Seward, Alaska. Benny had had a tragic **upbringing**. His mother died when he was just three years old. Soon after the family's house had burned down. Benny's father put his two sons in an orphanage and sent his daughter to a school in Oregon.

Benny's design showed what he thought and felt about Alaska. Benny explained the scene for the judges: "The blue field is for the Alaska sky and the forget-me-not, an Alaskan flower. The North Star is for the future of the state of Alaska, the most northerly in the Union. The Dipper is for the Great Bear — **symbolizing** strength."

Benny Benson (1913~1972)

Benny's design was chosen from among all the others. That design became the pattern for the flag that now flies over Alaska, which has become the 49th state of the United States.

Did you know?

The United States purchased Alaska from Russia in 1867 at the price of $7.2 million.

Reading Activites

MAIN IDEA

1. What is the story mainly about?

    a The story behind the design of the Alaskan flag

    b Many designs shown in the Alaskan flag design competition

    c The schoolchildren who designed the Alaskan flag

DETAILS

2. What is true according to the story?

    a Benny Benson was sent to a school in Oregon.

    b The Alaskan flag was designed by a 13-year-old boy.

    c Benny's flag showed how Alaska looked.

3. What is NOT true according to the story?

    a The blue field in the Alaskan flag was for the Alaska sky and an Alaskan flower.

    b The North Star in the flag represented Alaska's future.

    c The Dipper in the flag represented the giant Atlantic salmon.

4. What does it mean that Alaska was just a territory in 1927?

    a It was yet to become a state and gain the rights of US states.

    b It was a different territory, not linked to the US.

    c It was US territory with the same rights as other US states.

CONTEXT CLUES

5. What does the word *orphanage* mean in the sentence below?
Benny lived in an <u>orphanage</u> *in Seward, Alaska.*

    a a family living together in one building

    b a place where a person lives

    c a place where children without parents can live

Thinking & Writing

A. Developing Logical Thinking Skills

Visualizing as You Read

We can understand something better by visualizing it. We can think about what something looks like. We can also imagine how unique its shape is.

What can you visualize when reading the following sentence?

1. Soon after the family's house had burned down.
A house which was _____.

a destroyed by a fire   b rebuilt by a rich family

2. The blue field is for the Alaska sky.
The Alaska sky, whose color is _____.

a anything but blue   b really blue

B. Developing Writing Skills

Based on the model passage below, write a story about how Alaska's flag was designed.

Alaska's flag was designed by a 13-year-old schoolboy. The boy who designed it had had a tragic childhood. His design showed what he thought and felt about Alaska. It is still used today.

Your Turn

Alaska's flag _____. The boy who designed it _____.

His design _____. It is _____.

Women's Suffrage

1 Kate Sheppard (1847~1934)

Thinking Aloud

Look at the picture above and answer the following questions.

1. What is this a picture of?
2. Whose pictures are on the money in your country?

Words in Passage

Match the word with its definition.

_____ **1.** equal   ⓐ to choose someone by special ways

_____ **2.** generation   ⓑ a period of ten years

_____ **3.** election   ⓒ having the same rights as everyone else

_____ **4.** decade   ⓓ an act of voting to select someone for a public office

_____ **5.** vote   ⓔ a group of people born and living during the same time

Women's Suffrage

In most countries, women today have the same **voting** rights as men. In fact, voting rights are something that most women take for granted. But this hasn't always been the case. Women's suffrage — in other words, women's voting rights — was something that was fought for by **generations** of women before us.

Women's suffrage became an important issue in the late 19th century. In 1893, New Zealand became the first country in the world to give women the same voting rights as men. New Zealand introduced universal suffrage — **equal** voting rights for all adults — after about two **decades** of campaigning by suffragettes, or women fighting for the right to vote in national **elections**. The suffragettes said that female voting would improve politics. People against these women said that women belonged in the home, taking care of their family, not in politics.

Kate Sheppard was the most famous member of the New Zealand women's suffrage movement. Sheppard was a powerful speaker and organizer. Her work had a great impact on women's suffrage movements in other countries, including Australia, England, Canada, and the United States. Today she is New Zealand's most well-known suffragette and appears on its ten-dollar note.

Did you know?

In 1992, Edmund Hillary appeared on the five-dollar note of New Zealand. He was the first man that conquered Mount Everest.

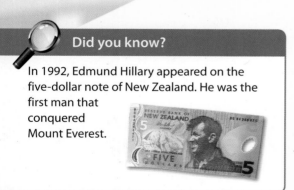

Reading Activites

MAIN IDEA **1.** What is the story mainly about?

  (a) Women gaining the right to vote in New Zealand

  (b) The morality of politics

  (c) Voting rights in the United States

DETAILS **2.** What is true according to the story?

  (a) Women gained the right to vote in New Zealand in 1883.

  (b) Kate Sheppard was a well-known New Zealand suffragette.

  (c) Everyone agreed that female voting would improve politics.

3. What is NOT true according to the story?

  (a) Most women take their right to vote for granted.

  (b) Kate Sheppard is on the New Zealand twenty-dollar note.

  (c) Generations of women fought for women's suffrage.

4. What does it mean that female voting would improve politics?

  (a) That politicians would behave better if women gained the right to vote

  (b) That more people would vote if elections existed

  (c) That men would play a greater role in taking care of the family

CONTEXT CLUES **5.** What does the phrase *take for granted* mean in the sentence below?
In fact, voting rights are something that most women <u>take for granted</u>.

  (a) to not know the importance of something

  (b) to say something false

  (c) to agree to do something

Thinking & Writing

A. Developing Logical Thinking Skills

Ask and Answer Your Own Questions

When you read a passage, ask yourself questions about the content. Then, find logical answers to your questions. That will help you to get important information from the passage.

After reading the following sentence, which question can you form?

1. Women's suffrage became an important issue in the late 19th century.

  a What stopped women from having voting rights before the 19th century?

  b Why did science develop so fast in the late 19th century?

2. The suffragettes said that female voting would improve politics.

  a Do women think highly of politics?

  b Why are women generally good at learning foreign languages?

B. Developing Writing Skills

Based on the model passage below, write a story about women's suffrage.

Women in New Zealand gained the right to vote before any other country. Kate Sheppard is New Zealand's most famous suffragette. She influenced women's suffrage movements in other countries. Today she is on New Zealand's ten-dollar note.

Your Turn

Women in New Zealand _____ . Kate Sheppard _____ .

She _____ . Today _____ .

America's First Woman Justice

Unit 04

1 Sandra Day O'conner   2 Barack Obama   3 Supreme Court

Thinking Aloud

Look at the picture above and answer the following questions.

1. What is the woman in the above picture doing?
2. In what situation do people usually have to do this?

Words in Passage

Match the word with its definition.

_____ **1.** court   ⓐ someone who may get an important job

_____ **2.** form   ⓑ the place where judges make legal decisions

_____ **3.** approve   ⓒ the highest law of a country or a state

_____ **4.** constitution   ⓓ to officially accept something

_____ **5.** candidate   ⓔ to start an organization

America's First Woman Justice

The United States Supreme **Court** is the highest court in the country. It was **formed** over 200 years ago. The United States has a very important law called the *US* **Constitution**. According to this special law, the Supreme Court is made up of nine justices, or judges. The justices meet in Washington D.C. and do serious jobs.

For a long time, only men became Supreme Court justices. But in 1981, Sandra Day O'Connor of Arizona became the first female Supreme Court justice. She began her work as a justice on September 25, 1981.

Becoming a Supreme Court justice is a long process. First, the President decides who is the right person to become a Supreme Court justice. Then, he or she asks Congress to **approve** the decision. In other words, the President asks Congress to allow him or her to appoint the **candidate** as a Supreme Court judge. After Congress approves the President's decision, the candidate finally becomes a Supreme Court justice.

Sandra Day O'Connor went through all that process. Before she became a Supreme Court justice, O'Connor worked in the field of politics. As a Supreme Court justice, she made many good decisions about important social issues. She retired with honor in 2006.

Did you know?

In 1967, Thurgood Marshall became the first African-American justice of the Supreme Court of the United States.

Reading Activites

1. What is the story mainly about?

   ⓐ How to become a US Supreme Court justice

   ⓑ Congress and the US Constitution

   ⓒ The appointment of the first female US Supreme Court justice

2. What is true according to the story?

   ⓐ There has always been a woman justice on the Supreme Court.

   ⓑ Sandra Day O'Connor became a Supreme Court justice in 1981.

   ⓒ Congress does not allow the President to choose male justices.

3. What is NOT true according to the story?

   ⓐ The Supreme Court was set up by the US Constitution.

   ⓑ There are twelve justices on the Supreme Court.

   ⓒ The Supreme Court meets in Washington, D.C.

4. Who needs to approve the President's decision about Supreme Court justices?

   ⓐ The US Constitution

   ⓑ The US Supreme Court

   ⓒ The US Congress

5. What does the word *field* mean in the sentence below?
O'Connor worked in the __field__ of politics.

   ⓐ an area of ground for sports

   ⓑ a type of furniture

   ⓒ an area of activity

Thinking & Writing

A. Developing Logical Thinking Skills

Retell and Summarize

In order to learn how to draw logical conclusions, you need to learn how to retell or summarize a reading passage in your own words.

Which answer best retells the following sentence?

1. Sandra Day O'Connor became the first female Supreme Court justice.

   ⓐ Sandra Day O'Connor set up the United States Supreme Court.

   ⓑ Sandra Day O'Connor was the first woman to become a Supreme Court justice.

2. Becoming a Supreme Court justice is a long process.

   ⓐ There are many steps to becoming a Supreme Court justice.

   ⓑ A large number of people want to become a Supreme Court justice.

B. Developing Writing Skills

Based on the model passage below, write a story about the US Supreme Court.

The US Supreme Court is the highest court in the nation. It was set up by the US Constitution and has nine justices. Sandra O'Connor was the first woman appointed to the Supreme Court.

Your Turn

The US Supreme Court _____. It _____.

Sandra O'Connor _____.

Unit 05

The Highest Point

1 Edmund Hillary   2 Tenzing Norgay   3 Jim Whittaker

Thinking Aloud

Look at the picture above and answer the following questions.

1. What is happening in this picture?
2. Have you ever climbed a great mountain? How did it make you feel?

Words in Passage

Match the word with its definition.

_____ **1.** unconquered   ⓐ a gas that is essential for life

_____ **2.** Sherpa   ⓑ to think about doing something

_____ **3.** consider   ⓒ with no one succeeding in climbing a mountain top

_____ **4.** huge   ⓓ a Himalayan person who often helps mountaineers

_____ **5.** oxygen   ⓔ very big or great

The Highest Point

TAR3-05
MP3

For mountain climbers, or *mountaineers*, the greatest adventure is reaching the top of Mount Everest in Nepal. Mount Everest is 8,847 meters high, making it the world's highest mountain.

Until 1953, Mount Everest stood **unconquered**. That year, the ninth British mountaineering group set out to attempt the first climb of the mountain. This time they were successful. A New Zealand climber, Edmund Hillary, and his Nepalese **Sherpa**, Tenzing Norgay, became the first climbers to reach the summit of Mount Everest.

Three years later, a Swiss mountaineering group successfully challenged Mount Everest. By this time, mountaineers from all over the world were **considering** attempting the challenge. Mountaineers in the United States were beginning to wonder when an American would stand "at the top of the world."

On May 1, 1963, Jim Whittaker of the United States and a fellow mountaineer from Nepal made an attempt to reach the summit of Mount Everest. These men struggled to overcome **huge** obstacles. Strong winds threatened to blow them off the mountain. At great heights it was necessary for them to breathe **oxygen** from tanks. They knew that one wrong step could cost them their lives.

Finally, at the summit of Mount Everest, Jim Whittaker placed an American flag. He was the first American to do so!

Did you know?

Junko Tabei became the first woman to conquer Mount Everest in 1975. Her college major was English literature.

Reading Activites

MAIN IDEA

1. What is the story mainly about?

    a Learning to reach the North Pole

    b Mountaineers who succeeded in reaching the summit of Mount Everest

    c Preparing to climb the highest mountain in the world

DETAILS

2. What is true according to the story?

    a Mount Everest was conquered for the first time by a British group.

    b Mount Everest is in the United States.

    c At great heights, mountain climbers cannot breathe at all.

3. What is NOT true according to the story?

    a Edmund Hilliary and Tenzing Norgay conquered Mount Everest in 1953.

    b Jim Whittaker reached the summit of Mount Everest in 1963.

    c Edmund Hilliary was part of a Swiss group.

4. Who was the first person to place an American flag on the summit of Mount Everest?

    a Tenzing Norgay

    b Jim Whittaker

    c Edmund Hillary

CONTEXT CLUES

5. What does the phrase *cost them their lives* mean in the sentence below?
They knew that one wrong step could <u>cost them their lives</u>.

    a to result in them falling and dying

    b to pay a lot of money

    c to result in them living in Nepal

Thinking & Writing

A. Developing Logical Thinking Skills

Skill Focus

Connect the Text to Your Prior Experiences

Connecting the text to your previous experiences is a great way to learn how to think logically. This is largely because logic is partly based on our everyday experiences.

Which can you connect the following <u>underlined subject</u> to?

1. <u>Mount Everest</u> is 8,847 meters high, making it the world's highest mountain.

    a A mountain where you can play with young children

    b A high mountain that is very difficult to climb

2. <u>Strong winds</u> threatened to blow them off the mountain.

    a Winds that can put your life in danger

    b Winds that can help you in hot weather

B. Developing Writing Skills

Based on the model passage below, write a story about Mount Everest.

Mount Everest is the world's highest mountain. Climbers from all over the world dream of reaching its summit. But it is a difficult mountain to climb, especially in bad weather. The first people to reach the summit of Mount Everest were Edmund Hillary and his Nepalese Sherpa, Tenzing Norgay.

Your Turn

Mount Everest _____. Climbers _____.

But _____. The _____.

Sky Pioneers

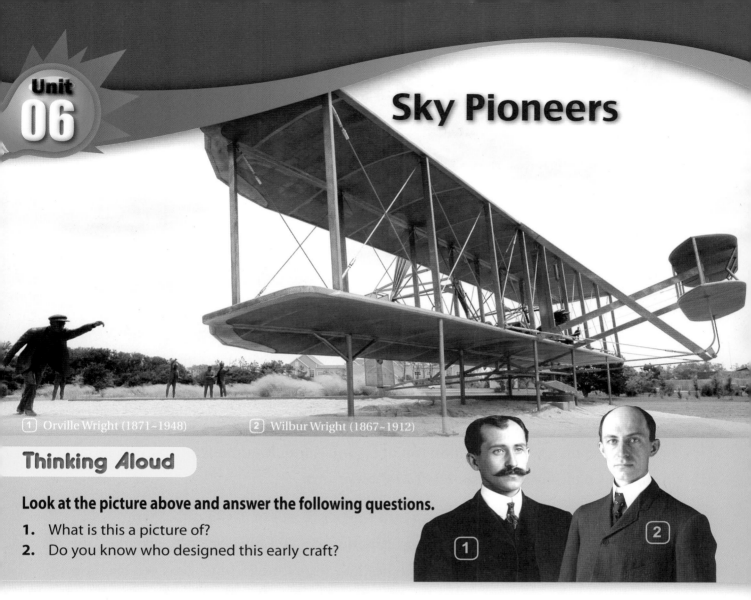

1 Orville Wright (1871~1948)　　2 Wilbur Wright (1867~1912)

Thinking Aloud

Look at the picture above and answer the following questions.

1. What is this a picture of?
2. Do you know who designed this early craft?

Words in Passage

Match the word with its definition.

_____ **1.** present   ⓐ a person who just watches an event

_____ **2.** observe   ⓑ to stop holding something

_____ **3.** onlooker   ⓒ to see something happen

_____ **4.** mean   ⓓ being in a particular place

_____ **5.** release   ⓔ to have something in your mind as a goal

Sky Pioneers

Air history was made at Kitty Hawk, North Carolina, on December 17, 1903. Few people were **present** to **observe** the exciting event. Those **onlookers** that were there wondered what the strange bicycle-makers from Dayton, Ohio, were up to now. There were no news reporters there to watch this important occasion. "People aren't **meant** to fly," some people said. They laughed when they heard what the Wright brothers were planning to do. They were sure that their flying experiment would be a failure.

This now-famous winter day was cold and windy. The odd-looking plane was placed on a wooden rail on top of a sand dune. It had a wingspan of about thirteen meters and only weighed 274 kilograms.

Orville Wright climbed bravely into the pilot's slot at 10:35 a.m. Lying facedown, he warmed up the motor. When it reached full power, the weak-looking plane shook a lot. The cable holding the plane in place was **released** and the strange-looking airplane moved down the sand track. Wilbur ran alongside the plane, steadying the wingtip. Up, up into the air the odd-looking plane flew. For twelve breathtaking seconds, the plane soared through the air. Then slowly and gently, controlled by the pilot, the plane landed on the sand. Man's first engine-powered flight was over. But the air age had just begun!

Did you know?

Neither Orville nor Wilbur married. They spent most of their lives developing airplanes.

Reading Activites

MAIN IDEA

1. What is the story mainly about?

- a The first engine-powered flight
- b How the first airplane was built
- c News reporters at Kitty Hawk

DETAILS

2. What is true according to the story?

- a Most reporters considered the flight on December 17, 1903, an important occasion.
- b The Wright brothers made their first flight in North Carolina.
- c Wilbur Wright piloted the first engine-powered flight.

3. What is NOT true according to the story?

- a Orville Wright flew the airplane for twelve seconds.
- b The Wright brothers' airplane weighed more than 300 kilograms.
- c The weather was cold on this day in history on December 17, 1903.

4. Why does the writer say that air history was made on December 17, 1903?

- a Because the airplane shook as Orville Wright took off.
- b Because people were sure that the flying experiment would be a failure.
- c Because the first engine-powered plane was successfully flown on this day.

CONTEXT CLUES

5. What does the word *slot* mean in the sentence below?
Orville Wright climbed bravely into the pilot's slot at 10:35 a.m.

- a a place or position in an organization
- b a period of time for a particular occurrence
- c a long, thin opening

Thinking & Writing

A. Developing Logical Thinking Skills

Skill Focus

Skip, Read On, and Go Back
Logical thinking skills ask you to understand the context of a given passage, which also helps you to guess the meanings of unfamiliar words.

What is the missing word in the following sentence?

1. Unfortunately, few people were _____ to observe the exciting event.

a absent

b present

2. For twelve breathtaking seconds, the plane _____ through the air.

a soared

b dropped

B. Developing Writing Skills

Based on the model passage below, write a story about the Wright brothers' first flight.

The Wright brothers flew the first engine-powered flight on December 17, 1903. Orville Wright piloted the flight and his brother, Wilbur, ran next to the plane to steady the wings. People laughed when they heard what the brothers were going to try to do. The day made history.

Your Turn

The Wright brothers _____. Orville Wright _____.

People _____. The day _____.

Birds that Fly in the Ocean

1 Galapagos Island Penguins   2 Galapagos Islands

Thinking Aloud

Look at the picture above and answer the following questions.

1. What is the above picture of?
2. Where do these animals like to live?

Words in Passage

Match the word with its definition.

_____ **1.** search   ⓐ working very well

_____ **2.** flap   ⓑ very warm, as in the the tropics

_____ **3.** efficient   ⓒ an amount of something covering a surface

_____ **4.** layer   ⓓ to look for something

_____ **5.** tropical   ⓔ to move wings up and down so as to fly

Birds that Fly in the Ocean

TAR3-07
MP3

Unlike most birds, penguins cannot fly in the air. Penguins spend almost 75 percent of their time underwater, **searching** for food in the ocean. When they are in the water, they dive and **flap** their wings. It looks like they are flying!

A penguin's body is built for the most **efficient** swimming. Underwater, penguins can move at about 25 kilometers per hour!

The only time when penguins are in the air is when they leap out of the water. They often do this to get air before diving back down for fish. Penguins cannot breathe underwater. However, they can hold their breath for a long time.

A penguin's body is covered with thick **layers** of small, soft feathers. A layer of fat under their skin called "blubber" helps penguins to keep warm in polar weather. Sometimes penguins need more than their feathers and blubber to keep warm, though. Often they will gather shoulder to shoulder with their wings tight against their bodies to keep each other warm. As many as 5,000 penguins will get together to warm each other up.

Penguins that live in warmer climates have the opposite problem. These penguins, such as the Galapagos Island penguins, live in such **tropical** weather that they become too hot. These penguins spread their wings out to help them cool off.

Did you know?

The Little Blue penguin is the smallest penguin species. On average, it is about 40 centimeters tall and weighs around 1 kg.

Reading Activites

MAIN IDEA

1. What is the story mainly about?

    a Penguins that live on the Galapagos Islands

    b The major features of penguins

    c Similarities beteen penguins and eagles

DETAILS

2. What is true according to the story?

    a Penguins are birds, but they cannot fly in the air.

    b Penguins spend about 50 percent of their time underwater.

    c Penguins spend much of their time in the air.

3. What is NOT true according to the story?

    a When penguins dive and flap their wings, it looks like they're flying.

    b All penguins live in very cold climates.

    c Penguins can move at about 25 kilometers an hour.

4. What does it mean that penguins sometimes need more than their feathers?

    a that they sometimes need things other than their feathers

    b that they sometimes need their feathers more than anything else

    c that they sometimes need to use their feathers more often

CONTEXT CLUES

5. What does the word *polar* mean in the sentence below?
Blubber helps penguins to keep warm in <u>polar</u> weather.

    a of very hot areas

    b of deserts

    c of very cold areas

Thinking & Writing

A. Developing Logical Thinking Skills

Direct and Indirect Information
To effectively develop logical thinking skills, you need to tell direct information from indirect information. Indirection information is almost the same as implied information.

1. What is directly stated in the following sentence?
   A penguin's body is built for the most efficient swimming.

   a A penguin's body is used to build the most efficient swimming pool.

   b The structure of a penguin's body is most efficient for swimming.

2. What is implied in the following sentence?
   Blubber helps penguins to keep warm in polar weather.

   a Penguins enjoy warm weather in the polar seas.

   b Keeping warm is important for surviving in polar weather.

B. Developing Writing Skills

Based on the model passage below, write a story about penguins.

I think penguins are interesting because they cannot fly although they are birds. They are in the air only when they leap out of the water. They usually live in very cold climates, but some penguins, such as the ones that live on the Galapagos Islands, are used to warmer temperatures.

Your Turn

I think penguins _____ . They _____ .

They _____ .

First Aid
for Snakebites

1 Rattlesnake

Thinking Aloud

Look at the picture above and answer the following questions.

1. Do you know what type of snake this is?
2. Have you ever seen a snake? How do you feel about snakes?

Words in Passage

Match the word with its definition.

_____ **1.** attack   **a** someone who has been hurt

_____ **2.** disapprove   **b** having something very harmful

_____ **3.** poisonous   **c** small living things that can cause disease

_____ **4.** victim   **d** to try to hurt or injure someone

_____ **5.** bacteria   **e** to disagree with someone's behavior

First Aid for Snakebites

TAR3-08
MP3

A rattlesnake feels threatened by nearby hikers. They get closer, and it raises its head, ready to **attack**. The hikers hear the familiar rattle noise rattlesnakes make when they feel the need to protect themselves. The **victim** of this **poisonous** attack falls to the ground. The man has been bitten on the leg. The snake goes away. His friend takes out a knife and cuts the bite mark out of the man's leg. He thinks that by doing this type of first aid, he will prevent the poison from spreading throughout the man's body.

The man's friends get him to a hospital. But the man's leg will never be the same again. He has lost much of its mobility. "The problem was not caused by the snakebite," the doctor tells the man. It was caused because his friend cut a nerve in his leg when trying to draw out the poison. People often give the wrong kind of first aid to snakebite victims.

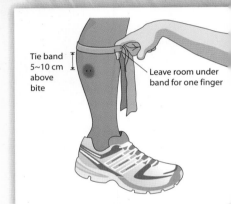

Tie band 5~10 cm above bite

Leave room under band for one finger

Perhaps you have heard you should suck the poison out of a snakebite, not cut it out. Many doctors **disapprove** of this type of first aid too because a person's mouth contains **bacteria**.

The man's friends should have calmed the man down, kept his leg as still as possible, and then gotten medical help for him quickly. They should not have tried to do first aid to a snakebite on their own.

Did you know?

The black mamba is sometimes known as the most dangerous snake species. But it usually avoids humans instead of attacking them.

Reading Activites

MAIN IDEA

1. What is the story mainly about?

a Where to take a victim of a snakebite

b How to cut the poison out of a snakebite

c The importance of giving correct first aid to snakebite victims

DETAILS

2. What is true according to the story?

a People often perform the wrong type of first aid on snakebite victims.

b There is nothing that can be done if a person is bitten by a poisonous snake.

c Many doctors agree that people should suck the poison out of a snakebite.

3. What is NOT true according to the story?

a You should cut the poison out of a snakebite with a knife.

b People shouldn't suck the poison out of a snakebite.

c All snakebite victims suffer from the knife cuts made to draw out poison.

4. What type of poisonous snake bit the man in this story?

a coral snake

b rattlesnake

c copperhead

CONTEXT CLUES

5. What does the word *mobility* mean in the sentence below?
He has lost much of its <u>mobility</u>.

a ability to move

b being weak and tired

c desire to move

Thinking & Writing

A. Developing Logical Thinking Skills

Skill Focus

Drawing Logical Conclusions

The ability to draw logical conclusions from a given passage is difficult to develop. To do that, you need to think carefully about the details given in the passage.

Decide if the <u>underlined conclusion below</u> is based on the details offered to you.

1. A rattlesnake feels threatened by nearby hikers. <u>Therefore, it welcomes the hikers</u>.

   ⓐ Yes   ⓑ No

2. The victim of this poisonous attack falls to the ground. <u>Therefore, the victim must feel a sharp pain</u>.

   ⓐ Yes   ⓑ No

B. Developing Writing Skills

Based on the model passage below, write a story about snakebite first aid.

Snakebite first aid is something many people get wrong. Some people think they should cut into the snakebite to prevent the poison from spreading throughout the victim's body. Other people think the poison should be sucked out of the snakebite. But doctors advise against doing both these things.

Your Turn

Snakebite first aid _____. Some people think _____.

Other people think _____. But _____.

Lights, Camera, Woof!

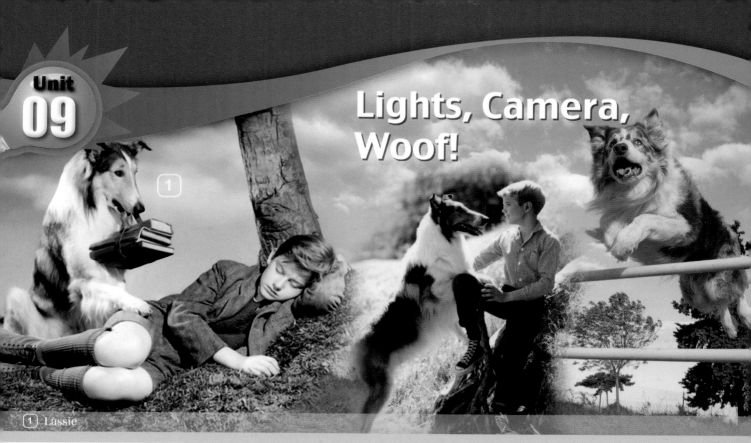

① Lassie

Thinking Aloud

Look at the picture above and answer the following questions.

1. What are the above pictures of?
2. What other dog actors can you think of?

Words in Passage

Match the word with its definition.

_____	**1.** perform	**a**	always supporting someone
_____	**2.** admire	**b**	taking a lot of time to do
_____	**3.** envy	**c**	to act a play or play a piece of music
_____	**4.** time-consuming	**d**	to respect and like someone or something
_____	**5.** loyal	**e**	to want to have another person's things

Lights, Camera, Woof!

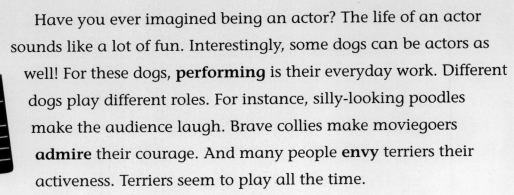

Have you ever imagined being an actor? The life of an actor sounds like a lot of fun. Interestingly, some dogs can be actors as well! For these dogs, **performing** is their everyday work. Different dogs play different roles. For instance, silly-looking poodles make the audience laugh. Brave collies make moviegoers **admire** their courage. And many people **envy** terriers their activeness. Terriers seem to play all the time.

But performing dogs have had special training. This is because they sometimes have to do something dangerous. Therefore, performing dogs sometimes follow unusual orders. For example, trainers may order their dogs to leap through high windows. In such cases, however, the trainers do everything they can to protect their performing "actors."

Trainers must take good care of performing dogs. These people notice when their dogs feel too tired. They also know that training dogs is a difficult, **time-consuming** process. It cannot be done overnight. Therefore, these people are very kind and patient.

Lassie was a famous performing dog. He was a lead actor in a well-known show named for him: *Lassie*. The show ran from 1954 through 1973. Throughout the show, Lassie remained **loyal** to his co-actor, Timmy. Lassie was always ready to help his best friend Timmy.

Did you know?

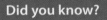

Dogs can hear sounds within the frequencies of 40 Hz to 60,000 Hz, while people can hear sounds within the frequencies of 20 Hz to 20,000 Hz.

Reading Activites

MAIN IDEA

1. What is the story mainly about?

(a) Performing dogs

(b) Many different dogs that draw special attention

(c) *Lassie* from the famous TV show

DETAILS

2. What is true according to the story?

(a) Performing dogs are naturally good at acting.

(b) Special training prepares performing dogs for something dangerous.

(c) Trainers do not care about their performing dogs.

3. What is NOT true according to the story?

(a) Collies are often described as brave in movies.

(b) Silly-looking poodles are used to make the audience feel sad.

(c) Performing dogs must learn to follow unusual orders.

4. What does it mean that it cannot be done overnight?

(a) It takes a long time to do it.

(b) People usually do not work at night.

(c) You should not cook food for too long.

CONTEXT CLUES

5. What does the word *courgage* mean in the sentence below?
Brave collies make moviegoers admire their <u>courage</u>.

(a) being lazy

(b) being busy

(c) being brave

Thinking & Writing

A. Developing Logical Thinking Skills

Skill Focus

Finding Out What an Expression Refers To
Using logic involves recognizing certain objects. Therefore, it is important to find out what a particular expression refers to.

Decide what each <u>underlined expression</u> below refers to.

1. Some dogs can be actors. Performing is <u>their</u> daily work.

    a   Some cats   b   Some dogs

2. Trainers must take good care of performing dogs. <u>These people</u> notice when their dogs feel too tired.

    a   Trainers   b   Care and knowledge

B. Developing Writing Skills

Based on the model passage below, write a story about performing dogs.

Performing dogs appear in movies, television shows, and advertisements. They get special training to learn to perform dangerous things. Dog trainers need to show their animals great patience and kindness.

Your Turn

Performing dogs _____. They _____.

Dog trainers _____.

Mail Carriers of the Past

1. Benjamin Franklin Post Office

Thinking Aloud

Look at the picture above and answer the following questions.

1. What can you see in this picture?
2. Where do you think this man is riding to? Why?

Words in Passage

Match the word with its definition.

_____ **1.** trail

_____ **2.** overland

_____ **3.** port

_____ **4.** mail

_____ **5.** reliable

ⓐ a town or city where ships stop to load and unload cargo

ⓑ a path through a forest or a field

ⓒ able to be depended on

ⓓ letters or packages sent from one person to another

ⓔ on or across land

Mail Carriers of the Past

For a long time, Great Britain ruled America. These long periods are called Colonial times. During Colonial times, America was a British colony. The word *colony* means "a country which is ruled by a stronger country." In Colonial America, sending letters was not easy at all.

At first, people asked travelers to carry letters. Unfortunately, not many letters moved **overland**. This was because land travel was very dangerous because of hard-to-follow **trails** and poor roads.

As a result, ship owners began to carry letters for other people. These ship owners sailed up and down the Atlantic Coast. When their ships arrived in **port**, the ship owners would take the **mail** to a small hotel. Then, some people came by and claimed letters that had been written to them.

As America grew bigger, people wanted to find a more **reliable** way of sending letters. In 1672, people on horseback began to carry mail between Boston and New York. These people, called *postriders*, used the Boston Post Road. The road was made longer.

But using the post road to carry letters was not that reliable. Postriders did not like their jobs very much, and they often opened and read letters. Sometimes, letters were even stolen.

In 1753, Benjamin Franklin became the head of the Colonial postal system. He made great efforts to make the system more reliable. In 1775, Franklin became the first United States Postmaster General.

Did you know?

From April 3, 1860 to October 24, 1861, the Pony Express delivered mail from Missouri across the Great Plains to California on horseback.

Reading Activites

MAIN IDEA

1. What is the story mainly about?

   (a) How mail was delivered in Colonial America

   (b) The development of the United States as a strong country

   (c) A reliable postal system for Great Britain

DETAILS

2. What is true according to the story?

   (a) The Boston Post Road was built in the early 1600s.

   (b) During Colonial times, land travel was not safe due to poor roads.

   (c) Early mail services were very reliable.

3. What is NOT true according to the story?

   (a) Franklin became postmaster general in 1853.

   (b) As America grew, a more dependable way of sending letters was needed.

   (c) Ship owners took letters to small hotels.

4. Why was post road mail service unreliable?

   (a) Because postriders were diligent people.

   (b) Because postriders often opened and read letters.

   (c) Because postriders found it difficult to find places.

CONTEXT CLUES

5. What does the word *efforts* mean in the sentence below?
*He made great **efforts** to make the system more reliable.*

   (a) decisions to play more often

   (b) feelings shared by two people

   (c) serious work done by someone

Thinking & Writing

A. Developing Logical Thinking Skills

Recognizing Cause-and-Effect Relationships
Two different events can be connected to each other in many different ways. One of the ways is that one thing causes the other to occur. This is called a *cause-and-effect* relationship.

Decide if there is a cause-and-effect relationship between A and B.

1. **A:** Few people were willing to carry letters in Colonial America.
B: It was very difficult to send a letter in Colonial America.

(a) Yes   (b) No

2. **A:** America continued to grow and more people began to send letters to each other.
B: People did not believe that a more reliable way of sending letters was needed.

(a) Yes   (b) No

B. Developing Writing Skills

Based on the model passage below, write a story about the postal system in Colonial America.

The postal system in Colonial America wasn't reliable. At first, it relied on the few people who traveled overland. Later, the Boston Post Road was built and postriders carried mail between different cities. But mail would get opened, and sometimes it was even stolen.

Your Turn

The postal system in Colonial America _____ . At first, _____ .

Later, _____ . But _____ .

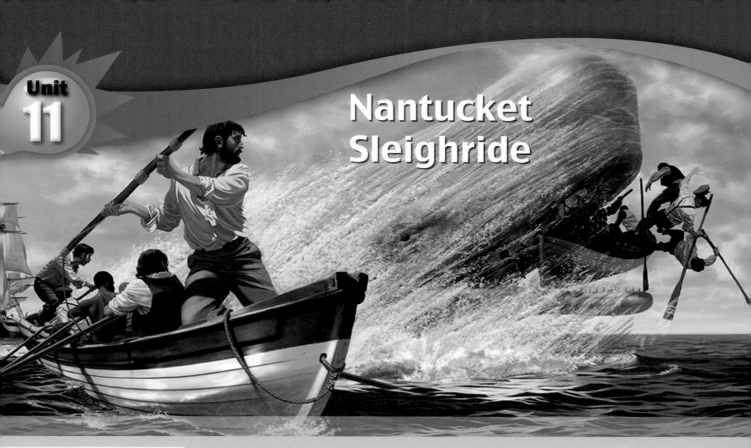

Nantucket Sleighride

Thinking Aloud

Look at the picture above and answer the following questions.

1. What can you see in the picture above?
2. What do you think the men are doing to the whale in the picture?

Words in Passage

Match the word with its definition.

_____ **1.** lad

_____ **2.** thrill

_____ **3.** steer

_____ **4.** drag

_____ **5.** race

a to move very fast

b a boy or young man

c to pull something somewhere

d to control the direction in which something moves

e a very exciting experience

Nantucket Sleighride

TAR3-11
MP3

There were many whaling ships on Nantucket Island, Massachusetts, in the late 1700s. Those ships were used to hunt whales. Young **lads** knew little about whaling, but many of them worked for the whaling ships. These lads, who were called greenhands, did not earn much money. But they got **thrills** from hunting whales. One of those thrills was a "Nantucket sleighride."

Whaling ships had whaling boats, which were small. When someone on a whaling ship found whales, the whaling boats were placed on the water. Five men in each boat rowed quickly toward the whales. Usually, someone in the back of the boat **steered**. People in the front of the boat attacked the whales by using something sharp.

If the thing hit the whales, they would **race** across the water. As a result, people in the boats were pulled by the animals. In a sense, the people were **dragged** by whales. This was called a "Nantucket sleighride." The ride might last for many hours depending on the kinds of whales. Some whales dragged people for a very long time.

In most countries, people cannot hunt whales anymore because many countries try to protect them. Unfortunately, Japan, Iceland, and Norway still hunt and kill whales.

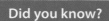
Did you know?

Many whale species, such as fin whales and humpback whales, have large brains and are known to be very intelligent.

48

Reading Activites

MAIN IDEA

1. What is the story mainly about?

   a Whales dragging people behind them in the whaling boats

   b A place called Nantucket, Massachusetts

   c Sleighrides on the snow in Nantucket, Massachusetts

DETAILS

2. What is true according to the story?

   a Greenhands knew little about whaling.

   b There were always ten men on each whaling boat.

   c Usually, someone in the front of the whaling boat steered.

3. What is NOT true according to the story?

   a Whaling was popular in Nantucket, Massachusetts, in the late 1700s.

   b Japan does not hunt or kill whales.

   c In most countries, whaling is not allowed.

4. What does it mean that they got thrills from hunting whales?

   a They did not really want to hunt and kill whales.

   b They got excited when they were hunting whales.

   c They got bored when they were on whaling ships.

CONTEXT CLUES

5. What does the phrase *depending on* mean in the sentence below?
The ride might last for many hours <u>depending on</u> the kinds of whales.

   a liked by many people

   b chosen by wise people

   c decided by something else

Thinking & Writing

A. Developing Logical Thinking Skills

Skill Focus

Comparing and Contrasting

When you try to understand two different things, it is a great idea to compare and contrast them. Try to find the similarities and differences between them.

Decide which statement about greenhands and whalers is correct.

1. Greenhands knew little about whaling, while whalers knew everything about it.

    a Greenhands had the same experiences as whalers.

    b Greenhands had little knowledge of whaling, unlike whalers.

2. Both greenhands and whalers tried to hunt large whales.

    a Greenhands and whalers had different goals.

    b Greenhands and whalers had the same goal.

B. Developing Writing Skills

Based on the model passage below, write a story about the Nantucket sleighride.

The Nantucket sleighride sounds exciting. I think being dragged behind a whale in a small boat must have been dangerous. I am happy whaling is no longer allowed in most countries. I feel sad when I think about the whales which have been killed.

Your Turn

The Nantucket sleighride _____. I think _____.

I _____. I _____.

Forgotten Inventions

① Benjamin Franklin (1706~1790)　　② Armonica

Thinking Aloud

Look at the picture above and answer the following questions.

1. What do you think these pictures are of?
2. Do you want to invent something new?

Words in Passage

Match the word with its definition.

_____	**1.** platform	**ⓐ**	parts that create the basic shape of something
_____	**2.** park	**ⓑ**	a usually raised structure that has a flat surface
_____	**3.** frame	**ⓒ**	to connect an object to another
_____	**4.** attach	**ⓓ**	a round object
_____	**5.** globe	**ⓔ**	to leave a car in a particular place

Forgotten Inventions

TAR3-12
MP3

In 1926, an unusual car was invented to solve **parking** problems. This small car did not weigh as much as other usual cars. There was a flat **platform** across the back of this car. Small wheels were **attached** to the platform. When a driver wanted to park his car, he just needed to move it to a nearby place. It was very easy to move the car to its parking space!

Some people wear metal bars on their legs. These bars help them to walk better. In 1886, special metal bars were invented for little children. These bars were for children who just began to walk. They had metal **frames** in them, and children could walk freely without worrying about falling down. Parents could also attach toys to the metal bars. These special metal bars were not popular among children, though. As a result, they were forgotten very quickly.

In the 1760s, Benjamin Franklin invented the *armonica*, or glass harmonica. This musical instrument contained a rod and glass **globes**. When people touched the globes, they made musical sounds. The sounds were beautiful, and many famous composers wrote music for the armonica. Although it is forgotten completely these days, the armonica was once a popular invention.

Did you know?

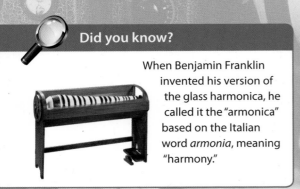

When Benjamin Franklin invented his version of the glass harmonica, he called it the "armonica" based on the Italian word *armonia*, meaning "harmony."

52

Reading Activites

MAIN IDEA

1. What is the story mainly about?

    a Inventions people no longer use

    b Interesting ideas for the future

    c Different ways to manage space

DETAILS

2. What is true according to the story?

    a Parking problems did not exist in 1926.

    b The special metal bars were invented for little children.

    c The special metal bars were invented in 1986.

3. What is NOT true according to the story?

    a Benjamin Franklin invented the *armonica*.

    b Many famous musicians composed music for the armonica.

    c The armonica contained many square-shaped boxes.

4. What does it mean that the armonica was once a popular invention?

    a The armonica was not popular anymore.

    b The armonica continues to be popular among inventors.

    c The armonica was invented by a famous person.

CONTEXT CLUES

5. What does the word *freely* mean in the sentence below?
Children could walk <u>freely</u> without worrying about falling down.

    a not controlled

    b in a way that is easy to make

    c while alone

Thinking & Writing

A. Developing Logical Thinking Skills

> ### Skill Focus
>
> **Recognizing the Speaker's / Writer's Intention**
> Sometimes, we can draw logical conclusions based on the writer's intention. This is because such intentions reflect the real meaning of the writer's statement.

Decide what the writer's intention is when he or she makes the following statement.

1. It was very easy to move the car to its parking space!

   a To say that the car had few parkign problems

   b To say that the owner of the car was very strong

2. Many famous composers wrote music for the armonica.

   a To say that many composers became famous because of the armonica

   b To say that many musicians accepted the armonica as a good instrument

B. Developing Writing Skills

Based on the model passage below, write a story about forgotten inventions.

I am glad that the world has creative people who invent things. Some of these things turn out to be very helpful. Others become forgotten. I think there must be lots of interesting forgotten inventions.

Your Turn

I _____ . Some _____ .

Others _____ . I think _____ .

Bat Talk!

1 Vampire Bat   2 Count Dracula   3 Bat Eating Fruit

Thinking Aloud

Look at the picture above and answer the following questions.

1. What is this a picture of?
2. Have you ever seen one of these animals before?

Words in Passage

Match the word with its definition.

_____	**1.** reputation	**a**	everything that exists in a particular environment
_____	**2.** ecosystem	**b**	what people think about someone or something
_____	**3.** control	**c**	to say what someone or something is like
_____	**4.** harmful	**d**	to limit the amount or growth of something
_____	**5.** describe	**e**	causing damage or harm

Bat Talk!

TAR3-13
MP3

Many people have a fear of bats. But like most animals, they play an important role in our **ecosystem**.

Bats help to **control harmful** insects. One large bat colony, which usually contains about 30,000 bats, would eat about 19 million mosquitoes a night! Bats also eat hundreds of thousands of insects that might otherwise damage or kill crops. But not all bats live in caves with other bats. Some of them live by themselves.

So if bats are so helpful to people, why do these poor-sighted, winged mammals have such a bad **reputation**?

One bat specialist says, "Part of the reason why people don't care for bats is that bats are rarely shown as cute animals in books or movies."

Other specialists agree. They say that, unlike how they are **described** in books and movies, bats don't attack people. In fact, experts point out that most bats are shy.

Dracula movies have probably done the most harm to this winged creature's reputation. "Thanks to the Count," says one expert referring to Count Dracula, "many people think all bats are bloodsucking vampires."

Although vampire bats do exist, they only live in the tropics, and they are more fond of animal blood than human blood. Other types of bats, which live elsewhere, eat either fruits or insects.

Did you know?

Unlike other gliding mammals, bats are the only mammals that can truly fly long distances.

Reading Activites

MAIN IDEA

1. What is the story mainly about?

(a) Count Dracula and vampire bats

(b) Various types of bats

(c) The reputation of bats compared with the real facts about them

DETAILS

2. What is true according to the story?

(a) Count Dracula has positively affected the reputation of bats.

(b) There is no such thing as vampire bats.

(c) Some bats live in colonies of about 30,000 bats.

3. What is NOT true according to the story?

(a) Bats play an important role in our ecosystem.

(b) Bats often attack people.

(c) Bats help to reduce the number of harmful insects.

4. How do bats help the ecosystem?

(a) By eating insects

(b) By sucking blood from animals

(c) By living in large groups in caves

CONTEXT CLUES

5. What does the word *specialists* mean in the sentence below?
Other specialists agree.

(a) experts in the field

(b) people who like bats

(c) special insects

Thinking & Writing

A. Developing Logical Thinking Skills

Applying Logic

Learning to apply logic is basically learning to make sound judgments about relationships between different sentences. Try to use your common sense and the details given in a reading passage.

Decide if the following sentences are connected naturally to each other.

1. Like most animals, bats play an important role in our ecosystem. So, we need to reduce their number.

    (a) Yes   (b) No

2. Bats don't attack people. So, we don't have to be afraid of them.

    (a) Yes   (b) No

B. Developing Writing Skills

Based on the model passage below, write a story about bats.

Many people have a fear of bats. Bats are usually shown in a bad light in movies and books. This has given them a bad reputation and is likely why so many people dislike them. But in reality, most bats do not suck blood. Most bats eat fruits and insects.

Your Turn

Many people _____. Bats _____.

This _____. But _____. Most _____.

Unit 14

An Island Rises from the Sea

1 Surtsey Island   2 Tsunami

Thinking Aloud

Look at the picture above and answer the following questions.

1. What is happening in the above picture?
2. Are there any volcanoes in your country?

Words in Passage

Match the word with its definition.

_____	**1.** disaster	ⓐ	the source or cause of something
_____	**2.** wipe	ⓑ	a group of people who live in the same area
_____	**3.** community	ⓒ	something that causes much suffering
_____	**4.** volcanic	ⓓ	to destroy something completely
_____	**5.** origin	ⓔ	caused by a volcano

An Island Rises from the Sea

For some people, the ocean suddenly seemed to be alive off the coast of Iceland. It threw lava, steam, and rocks up in the air. That was because a volcano had erupted on the seabed 110 meters below. Surprisingly, an island — 10 meters high and 180 meters long — appeared above the water. The year was 1963.

The new island, known today as Surtsey, grew bigger — 180 meters high and 1.6 kilometers long — within six months. New land was born thanks to a volcano.

Not many people believe that volcanoes are helpful. They think volcanoes lead to **disaster**. When a volcano erupts, it spreads fire and lava over surrounding areas. Very often, many people lose their lives. Sometimes, an entire city is **wiped** off the map.

When a volcano erupts at sea, it can cause giant waves called tsunamis. Tsunamis can destroy many **communities** which are hundreds of kilometers away from the volcano.

But sometimes, volcanoes can be helpful, and they can add an island to a map, as in the case of Surtsey. In fact, many islands are formed by the help of volcanoes. For example, Hawaii and the Aleutian Islands in Alaska are **volcanic** in **origin**. Maybe another volcano can add an island to the Earth.

Did you know?

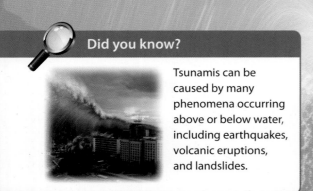

Tsunamis can be caused by many phenomena occurring above or below water, including earthquakes, volcanic eruptions, and landslides.

Reading Activites

MAIN IDEA

1. What is the story mainly about?

- (a) The adventure of exploring volcanoes
- (b) The birth of a volcanic island
- (c) The harmful effects of volcanoes on humans

DETAILS

2. What is true according to the story?

- (a) Many people consider volcanoes to be helpful to them.
- (b) People cannot live on islands caused by volcanic eruptions.
- (c) Surtsey Island is a volcanic island off the coast of Iceland.

3. What is NOT true according to the story?

- (a) Volcanic islands are not added to regular maps.
- (b) Surtsey Island first appeared in 1963.
- (c) People are often killed due to volcanic eruptions.

4. Why does the writer say that the ocean suddenly seemed to be alive?

- (a) Because the waves in the ocean were very big.
- (b) Because there was a lot of activity in the ocean.
- (c) Because sea animals were moving very fast.

CONTEXT CLUES

5. What does the word *formed* mean in the sentence below?
Many islands are __formed__ by the help of volcanoes.

- (a) made
- (b) broken
- (c) surprised

Thinking & Writing

A. Developing Logical Thinking Skills

Finding Appropriate Connecting Words
When choosing connecting words, good writers think about the logical relationships between sentences.

Find the approprite word for connecting the two sentences in each passage given below.

1. Very often, people are killed. _____ , an entire city is wiped off the map.

   a Nevertheless

   b Furthermore

2. Not many people believe that volcanoes are helpful. _____ , they think volcanoes lead to disaster.

   a Otherwise

   b Quite the contrary

B. Developing Writing Skills

Based on the model passage below, write a story about volcanic islands such as Surtsey Island.

Volcanoes that erupt in the sea can create islands. Such events are thought to help people. Surtsey Island appeared in 1963 as the result of a volcanic eruption off Iceland. The creation of islands is a welcome result of volcanic eruption.

Your Turn

Volcanoes _____ . Such events _____ .

Surtsey Island _____ . The _____ .

Unit 15

Small but Noisy

1 Howler Monkey

Thinking Aloud

Look at the picture above and answer the following questions.

1. Do you know the type of monkey in this picture?
2. What other types of monkeys can you name?

Words in Passage

Match the word with its definition.

_____ **1.** bad-tempered   **a**   a large, brown, wild cat with black spots

_____ **2.** vivid   **b**   easily annoyed

_____ **3.** discomfort   **c**   the loud sound of a wild animal

_____ **4.** jaguar   **d**   very clear and detailed

_____ **5.** roar   **e**   a feeling of pain

Small but Noisy

TAR3-15
MP3

Have you heard of the title of "the world's noisiest animal"? Of course, there is no such title. But if there is one, the howler monkey is a strong competitor for that title. This monkey's voice can carry up to five kilometers.

Different people describe the howler's voice in different ways. One **vivid** description compares its voice to the sounds of **jaguars**. The jaguars are experiencing great **discomfort** and making loud sounds. Another description compares the howler's voice to the **roar** of hungry lions.

Despite its loud voice, the howler weighs only about nine kilograms. Then, how can the monkey make such loud sounds? Scientists explain that this animal has a very good "speaker" in its voice box.

You can usually hear its loud voice after sundown, late in the evening, and at dawn. Interestingly, howlers make loud sounds when a storm is approaching.

Howler monkeys usually live together in family groups. An old male howler acts as a leader of such a family group. Howlers do not like traveling to distant places.

Do you think about keeping howlers as pets? Unlike other monkeys, they are **bad-tempered**, and they get angry very easily. Besides, they are not as smart as other monkeys.

Did you know?

Some Mayan tribes thought of howler monkeys as gods and worshipped their long, beautiful tails.

Reading Activites

MAIN IDEA

1. What is the story mainly about?

    a   Major features of the howler monkey

    b   Scientists who study howler monkeys

    c   Why howler monkeys are so angry

DETAILS

2. What is true according to the story?

    a   Howler monkeys make very gentle sounds.

    b   Howler monkeys are very noisy animals.

    c   Howler monkeys can weigh as much as ninety kilograms.

3. What is NOT true according to the story?

    a   Some people think the howler monkey's voice sounds like the roar of a hungry lion.

    b   You can hear the howler's loud voice when a storm is coming.

    c   Howlers are usually noisiest at noon.

4. What does it mean that an old male howler acts as a leader of such a family group?

    a   Old male howlers do not like other members of their family groups.

    b   Old male howlers do not usually make loud sounds.

    c   Old male howlers determine important things about their family groups.

CONTEXT CLUES

5. What does the phrase *strong competitor* mean in the sentence below?
But if there is one, the howler monkey is a <u>strong competitor</u> for that title.

    a   an animal that has a good chance of winning that title

    b   an animal that refuses to take part in a competition

    c   a strong fighter for freedom

Thinking & Writing

A. Developing Logical Thinking Skills

Skill Focus

Inferencing

Making logical inferences is an important element of logical thinking skills. To make such inferences, think about the essential meaning of a statement.

What can we infer from the sentence given below?

1. Howlers do not like traveling to distant places.

  a Howlers do not like moving their body parts such as their arms and legs.

  b Howlers prefer staying in particular places to going to faraway places.

2. Unlike other monkeys, they are bad-tempered, and they get angry very easily.

  a It will be difficult for people to get along with howlers.

  b Howlers are well-known for being kind to their human masters.

B. Developing Writing Skills

Based on the model passage below, write a story about howler monkeys.

Howler monkeys are known to be very noisy monkeys. Their voices can be heard five kilometers away. Different people describe the noise that a howler makes differently. The howler monkey makes a big noise, but it is not very big itself, weighing only nine kiolgrams.

Your Turn

Howler monkeys _____ . Their _____ .

Different people _____ . The howler monkey _____ .

The Dancing Stallions

Thinking Aloud

Look at the picture above and answer the following questions.

1. What is the above picture of?
2. Have you ever ridden a horse? Did you like it?

Words in Passage

Match the word with its definition.

_____ **1.** apply   **a**   to make a gesture to tell someone to do something

_____ **2.** method   **b**   pieces of flesh you use to make a movement

_____ **3.** muscle   **c**   a way of doing something

_____ **4.** signal   **d**   requiring someone to follow rules

_____ **5.** strict   **e**   to use something in a particular situation

The Dancing Stallions

Have you ever heard the word *stallion*? This word means "an adult male horse." The Spanish Riding School of Vienna is an exciting place that trains stallions. The stallions that are trained by the school are called *Lippizaner stallions*.

The training at the school is very **strict**. Before the stallions are trained, however, they are allowed to have some fun time. After that time, the stallions learn good manners.

Riders of Lippizaner stallions are called *riding masters*. When they **signal** the horses, Lippizaner stallions take very complex steps. These signals are a secret **method** of communication between the stallions and riding masters. By using their legs, the riding masters usually **apply** some pressure to the horses.

Lippizaner stallions can make beautiful and exciting dance movements. There are even special names for their movements. The horses often dance to music.

But it is not easy for the horses to make such dance movements. In fact, they require great strength. Therefore, the riding masters train the stallions very hard. As a result, the horses can build strong leg **muscles**. Those muscles help the stallions to make amazing movements.

Under the skilled hands of experienced riders, the proud stallions leap and dance. They seem to be full of joy and excitement.

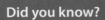

Did you know?

The Habsburg nobility helped the development of the Lippizaner breed in the 16th century.

Reading Activites

MAIN IDEA

1. What is the story mainly about?

    a The fact that riders signal horses by using pressure

    b The fact that many people watch rider and horse communicate

    c The fact that Lippizaner stallions and riders must have strict training

DETAILS

2. What is true according to the story?

    a Lippizaner stallions are trained in the Spanish Riding School of Vienna.

    b Lippizaner stallions are usually trained for one year.

    c Lippizaner stallions cannot perform complicated steps.

3. What is NOT true according to the story?

    a Lippizaner stallions often dance to music.

    b Lippizaner stallions have some fun time after their training begins.

    c Lippizaner stallions have strong leg muscles.

4. What can we infer from the sentence below?

There are even special names for their movements.

    a Their movements do not require any attention.

    b Their movements are dull and unexciting.

    c Their movements are unique and special.

CONTEXT CLUES

5. What does the word *amazing* mean in the sentence below?

Those muscles help the stallions to make <u>amazing</u> movements.

    a terrible

    b boring

    c impressive

Thinking & Writing

A. Developing Logical Thinking Skills

Skill Focus

Predicting Results

Sometimes, you need to predict the logical consequence of a particular situation. In such cases, think about how things tend to happen in real life.

What is the most likely result of the situation described in each sentence below?

1. These signals are a secret method of communication between the stallions and riding masters.

   a Viewers will not notice the use of these signals.

   b Viewers have been learning how to use these signals.

2. In fact, they require great strength.

   a Training programs will become unpopular among strong people.

   b Training programs will focus on improving physical strength.

B. Developing Writing Skills

Based on the model passage below, write a story about Lippizaners.

Lippizaner stallions and their riders train for many years to make their art look effortless. These horses train at a famous riding school in Vienna, Austria. For the first three years of their lives, these horses are allowed to play and enjoy their youth. But then they begin a long, intense training of manners, obedience, signaling, and so on.

Your Turn

Lippizaner stallions _____. These horses _____.

For the first three years _____. But _____.

Unit 17

Deep-Sea Adventure

1. Bathysphere (William Beebe)   2. Bathyscaphe   3. Deep-diving Submarine

Thinking Aloud

Look at the picture above and answer the following questions.

1. What is this a picture of?
2. What do you think this type of vehicle is used for?

Words in Passage

Match the word with its definition.

_____ **1.** accurately   **a** a ship that can work underwater

_____ **2.** maneuver   **b** free from mistakes and errors

_____ **3.** depths   **c** a remote area with few people living in it

_____ **4.** submarine   **d** the deepest parts of the sea

_____ **5.** frontier   **e** to move skillfully

Deep-Sea Adventure

TAR3-17
MP3

Over the years, explorers had made great efforts to **accurately** map the land and water surfaces of the Earth. But they failed to explore the ocean **depths**. In that sense, the ocean depths were an unexplored **frontier**. In the 1930s, some explorers tried to change that.

In 1930, William Beebe invented a special ship for underwater exploration. He called it a *bathysphere*. Beebe wanted to get deeper and deeper into the ocean. In 1934, Beebe succeeded in reaching a depth of over 3,000 feet. As time went by, this deep-diving ship succeeded in getting deeper into the ocean depths. In 1953, a deep-diving ship called a *bathyscaphe* successfully reached a depth of 10,300 feet. Seven years later, the bathyscaphe Trieste succeeded in reaching a depth of 35,800 feet.

Later, a deep-diving **submarine** was invented, which meant a new development in ocean exploration. The submarine is much better than the bathysphere and bathyscaphe in many ways. This deep-diving submarine can **maneuver** freely in the ocean depths. In addition, it can be used for various purposes, such as looking at cables and looking for sunken ships.

We are learning more and more about the ocean depths. For instance, we know that the ocean floor is not flat. We also know that millions of unusual animals live deep in the ocean depths. Someday, we will be able to find everything about the ocean depths.

Did you know?

On January 23, 1960, the Trieste reached the Challenger Deep in the Mariana Trench, which is the deepest part of the oceans of the Earth.

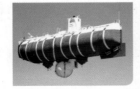

72

Reading Activites

MAIN IDEA

1. What is the story mainly about?

　(a) Deep-sea explorer William Beebe

　(b) Ocean depth exploration

　(c) Exploration of land and water surfaces

DETAILS

2. What is true according to the story?

　(a) At present, we do not know everything about the ocean depths.

　(b) The bathysphere worked much better than the bathyscaphe.

　(c) In 1934, Beebe reached a depth of more than 10,300 feet.

3. What is NOT true according to the story?

　(a) Undersea exploration was not made during the 1920s.

　(b) Great efforts were made to map the land surfaces of the Earth.

　(c) Deep-diving ships have several advantages over deep-diving submarines.

4. What does it mean that we are learning more about the ocean depths?

　(a) People have stopped talking about what is at the bottom of the ocean.

　(b) We are learning more about the landscape and animals of the deep ocean.

　(c) Scientists have found out everything about the ocean depths.

CONTEXT CLUES

5. What does the word *sunken* mean in the sentence below?
Submarines can be used to look for <u>*sunken*</u> *ships.*

　(a) fallen to the bottom of the ocean

　(b) floating on the surface of the ocean

　(c) destroyed completely in the ocean

Thinking & Writing

A. Developing Logical Thinking Skills

Guessing Hidden Ideas

Sometimes, writers do not clearly say something about their topic. This is because they believe readers already know it. But it is not always the case. So, you need to find hidden ideas in a reading passage by using logic.

What can be the hidden idea for each sentence below?

1. They failed to explore the ocean depths.

   a The ocean depths were interesting places.

   b The ocean depths were hard to explore.

2. Someday, we will be able to find everything about the ocean depths.

   a It will take a lot of time for us to completely understand the ocean depths.

   b It will be impossible for us to explore the ocean depths in the future.

B. Developing Writing Skills

Based on the model passage below, write a story about deep-sea exploration.

It is interesting to think that it is only the ocean depths that we have left to explore and map accurately. There are still a lot of underwater secrets to discover. More progress is sure to be made now that deep-diving submarines exist.

Your Turn

It is _____. There _____.

More _____.

A Dog's Best Friend

1 Cocker Pup   2 Collie Dog

Thinking Aloud

Look at the picture above and answer the following questions.

1. Can you tell the differences between the two dogs?
2. Do you enjoy playing with dogs?

Words in Passage

Match the word with its definition.

_____ **1.** fascinated

_____ **2.** adopt

_____ **3.** concerned

_____ **4.** pleading

_____ **5.** exhausted

a worried

b asking for something sincerely

c to accept

d very tired

e very interested in someone or something

A Dog's Best Friend

Tom and Jack were close friends. You might think they were two boys. But they were two dogs. Tom was a big collie, while Jack was a cocker pup. When Jack was very little, Tom **adopted** him. They lived happily together in Megan's house.

One day, Tom and Jack, together with Megan, went into a forest. The forest seemed to be shining brightly. **Fascinated** by its beauty, Jack forgot about following Tom. Jack barked happily at the surrounding trees and went out of sight. Barking worriedly, Tom tried to find Jack.

Tom came back to Megan, and she noticed that he seemed very **concerned**. Megan noticed the **pleading** in Tom's eyes. She followed Tom through the woods. At last, the dog stopped, and Megan saw Jack swimming dangerouly in a swamp.

Jack looked **exhausted**, but Megan tried to encourage him to get out of the swamp. But she couldn't think of diving into the swamp. At that very moment, Tom sprang into the swamp and approached Jack. Jack could catch Tom's collar and together they swam out of the swamp.

Megan felt relieved to know that both of her dogs were finally safe. Jack seemed to learn an important lesson, and he would not fail to follow Tom when going to unfamiliar places.

Did you know?

The term *cocker* refers to both the American cocker spaniel and the English cocker spaniel, which are hunting dogs.

Reading Activites

MAIN IDEA

1. What is the story mainly about?

    ⓐ A family that loves dogs

    ⓑ A friendship between two dogs

    ⓒ The dangers of forests for dogs

DETAILS

2. What is true according to the story?

    ⓐ The cocker pup's name was Tom.

    ⓑ Tom and Jack lived in Megan's house.

    ⓒ Jack never forgot to follow Tom.

3. What is NOT true according to the story?

    ⓐ The collie's name was Tom.

    ⓑ Jack fell into a swamp.

    ⓒ Megan swam toward Jack.

4. Why did Tom plead with Megan to follow him to the swamp?

    ⓐ Because his friend was in trouble.

    ⓑ Because his friend was hunted by an eagle.

    ⓒ Because his friend was playing hide-and-seek.

CONTEXT CLUES

5. What does the word *encourage* mean in the sentence below?
Megan tried to <u>encourage</u> him to get out of the swamp.

    ⓐ to make someone brave enough to do something

    ⓑ to stop someone from doing something

    ⓒ to respond happily to a request

Thinking & Writing

A. Developing Logical Thinking Skills

Telling Facts from Opinions

Logic is closely connected with facts. This is largely because logic is based on an objective understanding of facts. Therefore, it is very important to distinguish between facts and opinions.

Decide if each of the following sentences is a fact or an opinion.

1. Megan followed Tom through the woods.

   (a) a fact   (b) an opinion

2. The forest seemed to be shining brightly.

   (a) a fact   (b) an opinion

B. Developing Writing Skills

Based on the model passage below, write a story about Tom and Jack.

Tom acted like a big brother to Jack as soon as he began to live in Megan's house. Jack was young and playful, so when they went on a long walk in a new place one day, Jack became excited and ran off to explore. When he got into trouble, his friend Tom was there to help him.

Your Turn

Tom _____ . Jack _____ .

When _____ .

Mounties, Past and Present

1 Northwest Mounted Police   2 Royal Canadian Mounted Police

Thinking Aloud

Look at the picture above and answer the following questions.

1. What is this a picture of?
2. Do you know what country this picture would have been taken in?

Words in Passage

Match the word with its definition.

_____ **1.** dealings

_____ **2.** raging

_____ **3.** wilderness

_____ **4.** recruit

_____ **5.** dedication

a a wild and natural area where few people live

b when someone makes a great effort to do something

c someone who has just joined an organization

d moving with great force

e business activities or relationships with someone

Mounties, Past and Present

TAR3-19
MP3

A proud chapter in Canadian history began in 1874. Three hundred scarlet-coated men set out on horseback to bring law and order to a frontier **wilderness** that stretched from the Manitoba border to the Rocky Mountains. These men were members of the newly organized Northwest Mounted Police — the *Mounties*.

The Mounties soon gained the respect of both Indians and white settlers, through fair **dealings** with both groups. In their dealings with the Indians, the Mounties were polite and reliable. They also helped settlers fight prairie fires and **raging** floods. And the scarlet-coated Mounties kept law and order in the difficult days of the Klondike Gold Rush.

The Mounties of Canada's frontier days are now a distant memory. Today's Mounties make up a modern national police force called the *Royal Canadian Mounted Police*.

Mountie **recruits** are no longer required to learn to ride a horse or drive a dogsled; and the famous scarlet jacket is now worn only for special occasions. Planes, jeeps, and snowmobiles have replaced the dogsleds and horses. Brown uniforms and suits have replaced the scarlet jackets.

Their uniforms and crime-fighting techniques may have changed, but Mountie traditions remain the same. The Mounties are still recognized for their courage, **dedication** to duty, and skill in law enforcement. In the tracking down of criminals, today's Mounties share with earlier Mounties a reputation for "always getting their man."

Did you know?

In terms of total area, Canada is the second-largest country in the world, while it is the 36th most populous country.

Reading Activites

MAIN IDEA

1. What is the story mainly about?

    a The past and current Royal Canadian Mounted Police

    b The Canadian Federal Bureau of Investigation

    c The relationship between the Mounties and Canadian Indians

DETAILS

2. What is true according to the story?

    a Mountie recruits continue to learn how to drive a dogsled.

    b Today's mounties wear blue uniforms.

    c The first Mounties wore scarlet jackets.

3. What is NOT true according to the story?

    a The Mounties came to be highly regarded.

    b The Mounties earned recognition for their ability in law enforcement.

    c The original Mounties rode into a city.

4. What does it mean that the Mounties were polite and reliable?

    a The Mounties liked fighting violently with other people.

    b The Mounties did not deserve to be trusted.

    c The Mounties had good manners and could be trusted.

CONTEXT CLUES

5. What does the word *chapter* mean in the sentence below?
A proud <u>chapter</u> in Canadian history began in 1874.

    a a local member

    b a religious person

    c a particular period

Thinking & Writing

A. Developing Logical Thinking Skills

Understanding Imaginary Situations

When you try to draw logical conclusions, you should not confuse imaginary situations with real ones. Imaginary situations are usually described by such words as *would*, *could*, or *might*.

Decide if the following sentence describes an imaginary situation or a real one.

1. A frontier wilderness stretched from the Manitoba border to the Rocky Mountains.

   a an imaginary situation   b a real situation

2. Green uniforms could have replaced the scarlet jackets.

   a an imaginary situation   b a real situation

B. Developing Writing Skills

Based on the model passage below, write a story about Canada's Mounties.

The Royal Canadian Mounted Police were first established in 1874. They quickly gained the respect of both the Indians and the settlers. The original Mounties were known for their scarlet jackets. Today's Mounties aren't required to know how to ride a horse, and they no longer wear scarlet jackets, but they are still highly regarded by many people.

Your Turn

The Royal Canadian Mounted Police _____ .

They _____ . The original Mounties _____ .

Today's Mounties _____ .

No Strings or Wings

① Montgolfier Brothers' Balloon (1783)   ② Graf Zeppelin (1928)

Thinking Aloud

Look at the picture above and answer the following questions.

1. What are these pictures of?
2. Have you ever seen either of these before?

Words in Passage

Match the word with its definition.

_____ **1.** colorful   ⓐ the process of making something

_____ **2.** track   ⓑ something that can be burned to make energy

_____ **3.** production   ⓒ interesting and exciting

_____ **4.** far-off   ⓓ distant, far away in space

_____ **5.** fuel   ⓔ to search for a person or an animal

No Strings or Wings

TAR3-20
MP3

Balloons have played a **colorful** role in the story of flight. In 1783, a balloon containing hot air enabled people to fly for the first time. A short two years later, a balloon filled with hydrogen carried two men across the English Channel. From this time on, people began to dream of a day when balloons would provide passenger service to **far-off** places.

The *dirigible* was invented during the late 19th century. A balloon that was driven by motors, it could also be steered. Soon after, dirigibles designed to carry passengers were made.

It was Germany that took the lead in the **production** of passenger dirigibles. Built in Germany in 1928, the *Graf Zeppelin* became the most famous dirigible. In nine years, the Graf Zeppelin flew more than 1.6 million kilometers and carried thousands of passengers.

During the Second World War, a type of dirigible known as the *blimp* **tracked** down enemy submarines for the United States Navy. The US Navy went on to use blimps until as late as 1961.

But today, dirigibles have almost disappeared. They are slow and hard to handle. That said, there is some talk of bringing back dirigibles because they use little **fuel** and can carry large loads.

Although not dirigibles, other kinds of balloons remain in use. These balloons gather weather information and make scientific studies of high altitudes.

Did you know?

Filled with hydrogen and operated by a German company, the Graf Zeppelin made 590 flights from 1928 to 1937.

Reading Activites

MAIN IDEA

1. What is the story mainly about?

 ⓐ The history of the dirigible

 ⓑ Dangers of flying dirigibles

 ⓒ Blimps used by the United States Navy

DETAILS

2. What is true according to the story?

 ⓐ A dirigible is a balloon that can be steered.

 ⓑ The US was the leading producer of passenger dirigibles.

 ⓒ The *Graf Zeppelin* was built before 1900.

3. What is NOT true according to the story?

 ⓐ The United States Navy used blimps in World War II.

 ⓑ Dirigibles are widely used at the present time.

 ⓒ Today, balloons are used to obtain weather information.

4. Why might dirigibles be brought back?

 ⓐ Because they are slow and hard to handle.

 ⓑ Because they require little fuel and can transport large loads.

 ⓒ Because they can track down enemy submarines.

CONTEXT CLUES

5. What does the word *enabled* mean in the sentence below?
*In 1783, a balloon containing hot air **enabled** people to fly for the first time.*

 ⓐ to cause someone to be inactive

 ⓑ to make someone able to do something

 ⓒ to make something difficult

Thinking & Writing

A. Developing Logical Thinking Skills

Understanding Logic

The main role of logic is to allow your statement to express clear meaning. This is largely because logic makes it possible to naturally connect many different sentences.

Which of the following sentences can be logically connected to the sentence given below?

1. Soon after, dirigibles designed to carry passengers were made.

    a More and more people began to use dirigibles to travel to distant places.

    b People thought that dirigibles would be destroyed by forest fires.

2. But today, dirigibles have almost disappeared.

    a They are very convenient.   **b** They are too expensive to manage.

B. Developing Writing Skills

Based on the model passage below, write a story about dirigibles.

Dirigibles are balloons that are driven by motors and can be steered. They were designed in the late 19th century. After 1900, they were designed to carry passengers. The German-made Graf Zeppelin, which was built in 1928, was the most famous dirigible. Today, very few dirigibles are used.

Your Turn

Dirigibles _____. They _____.

After 1900, _____. The German-made Graf Zeppelin _____.

Today, _____.

Think About Reading

3

Reading

Workbook

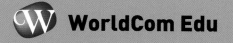
WorldCom Edu

Think About Reading

3

Workbook

Mystery Solved

A. Match each word to its definition.

_____ **1.** flesh

(a) when something is seen by people

_____ **2.** mainland

(b) the soft part of the body of an animal or person

_____ **3.** sighting

(c) the main area of land of a particular country

B. Choose the synonym of the underlined word in the sentence.

1. It is <u>common</u> for children to be curious.

(a) infrequent   (b) noble   (c) regular   (d) excellent

2. These days, becoming famous is <u>extremely</u> difficult.

(a) mildly   (b) normally   (c) insignificantly   (d) excessively

3. The way in which politics worked was always a <u>mystery</u> to her.

(a) understanding   (b) puzzle   (c) solution   (d) harmony

C. Fill in the blanks with the right expressions in the box.

account	concluded	mistaken

1. The report _____ that the government should spend more money on education.

2. Unfortunately, nothing can _____ for his strange behavior.

3. Sandra bought the product in the _____ belief that it would be good for her health.

D. Unscramble the words and write them in the blanks.

1. native / mainland / was / Guinea / and / to / New / Australia / it

_____ .

2. flesh-eating / named / its / back / animal / striped / was / for / this

_____ .

3. Tasmanian / became / how / been / extinct / a / the / always / mystery / has / tiger

_____ .

4. blame / extinction / tiger / are / for / of / to / humans / the / the / Tasmanian

_____ .

5. previously / that / it / been / out / disease / thought / tigers / had / wiped / by / the / was

_____ .

E. Listen to the recording and fill in each blank with a suitable word.

TAR3-01
MP3

The Tasmanian tiger had _____ become _____

rare on the Australian _____ before Europeans settled on the

_____ in 1788. But _____ of it remained _____

on the southern _____ of Tasmania _____ the 1800s. But

_____ 130 years, the animal _____ extinct in Tasmania

as _____ .

How Alaska Got Its Flag

A. Match each word to its definition.

_____ **1.** judge   ⓐ making you feel sad

_____ **2.** tragic   ⓑ unlike anyone or anything else

_____ **3.** unique   ⓒ someone who decides the winner in a contest

B. Choose the synonym of the underlined word in the sentence.

1. It took them a lot of time to <u>choose</u> a new house.

    ⓐ reject   ⓑ select   ⓒ dismiss   ⓓ delay

2. Surprisingly, many people entered the <u>contest</u> just for fun.

    ⓐ agreement   ⓑ unity   ⓒ competition   ⓓ accord

3. Most judges were amazed by her physical <u>strength</u>.

    ⓐ lack   ⓑ ignorance   ⓒ incompetence   ⓓ stamina

C. Fill in the blanks with the right expressions in the box.

explained	northerly	upbringing

1. The commander told his men to set off in a _____ direction.

2. Mark had a good _____, but he behaved very badly.

3. Michelle _____ the accident to the police officer.

D. **Unscramble the words and write them in the blanks.**

1. 1927, / did / flag, / it / still / Alaska / have / a / a / before / and / just / was / territory / not

_____.

2. design / to / used / Alaska's / winning / be / the / flag / planning / was / in

_____.

3. design / what / thought / Alaska / showed / felt / Benny's / and / about / he

_____.

4. explained / for / the / the / scene / Benny / judges

_____.

5. design / chosen / among / others / Benny's / the / from / was / all

_____.

E. **Listen to the recording and fill in each blank with a suitable word.**

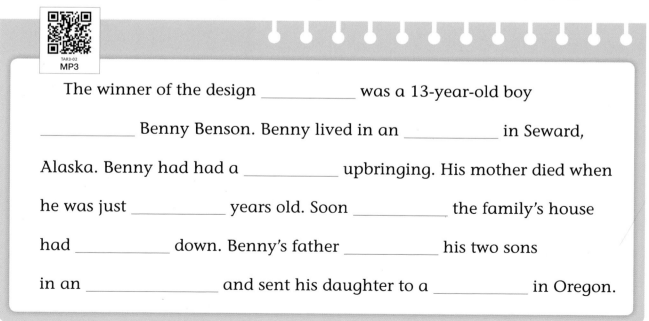

The winner of the design _____ was a 13-year-old boy

_____ Benny Benson. Benny lived in an _____ in Seward,

Alaska. Benny had had a _____ upbringing. His mother died when

he was just _____ years old. Soon _____ the family's house

had _____ down. Benny's father _____ his two sons

in an _____ and sent his daughter to a _____ in Oregon.

Women's Suffrage

A. Match each word to its definition.

_____ **1.** grant

_____ **2.** politics

_____ **3.** universal

ⓐ available for everyone

ⓑ to agree to give someone something

ⓒ activities having to do with gaining power in a country

B. Choose the synonym of the underlined word in the sentence.

1. Learning from the teacher had a big <u>impact</u> on my life.

ⓐ opportunity   ⓑ congestion   ⓒ effect   ⓓ conflict

2. Every effort has been made to <u>improve</u> their circumstances.

ⓐ diminish   ⓑ worsen   ⓒ weaken   ⓓ enhance

3. The President is the most <u>powerful</u> man in the United States.

ⓐ delicate   ⓑ influential   ⓒ feeble   ⓓ incapable

C. Fill in the blanks with the right expressions in the box.

case	issues	national

1. Laura raised some important _____ at the meeting.

2. It may be the _____ that we need more time to finish the work.

3. South Korea's _____ income has been increasing since 2010.

D. Unscramble the words and write them in the blanks.

1. countries, / today / same / as / rights / most / men / women / have / in / voting / the

   _____.

2. rights / that / women / granted / fact, / something / voting / most / for / take / in / are

   _____.

3. hasn't / been / case / always / the / this / but

   _____.

4. suffrage / important / the / an / women's / century / issue / late / in / became / 19th

   _____.

5. suffragettes / female / improve / that / the / politics / voting / said / would

   _____.

E. Listen to the recording and fill in each blank with a suitable word.

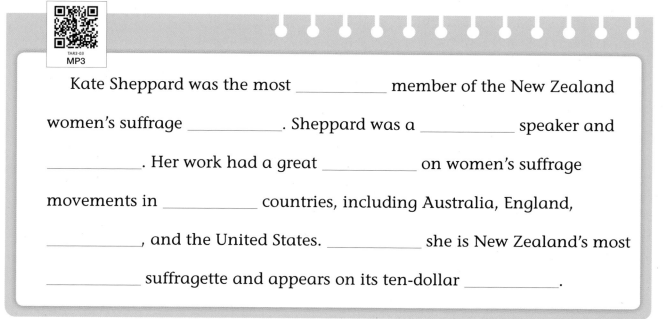

TAR3-03
MP3

Kate Sheppard was the most _____ member of the New Zealand

women's suffrage _____. Sheppard was a _____ speaker and

_____. Her work had a great _____ on women's suffrage

movements in _____ countries, including Australia, England,

_____, and the United States. _____ she is New Zealand's most

_____ suffragette and appears on its ten-dollar _____.

America's First Woman Justice

A. Match each word to its definition.

_____ **1.** Congress

_____ **2.** justice

_____ **3.** serious

ⓐ someone who makes legal decisions in a law court

ⓑ important and deserving a lot of thought

ⓒ the group of people in charge of making laws in the US

B. Choose the synonym of the underlined word in the sentence.

1. The officials <u>appointed</u> by the President remained loyal to him.

ⓐ designate   ⓑ disapprove   ⓒ retain   ⓓ require

2. The Senate decided to <u>approve</u> the agreement.

ⓐ oppose   ⓑ protest   ⓒ detest   ⓓ authorize

3. His poor health forced him to <u>retire</u> from public life.

ⓐ recruit   ⓑ depart   ⓒ defend   ⓓ advance

C. Fill in the blanks with the right expressions in the box.

finally	formed	process

1. We need to remember that scientific research is a slow _____.

2. After several meetings, the teachers _____ agreed on a solution.

3. Local farmers _____ an organization to protect their interests.

D. Unscramble the words and write them in the blanks.

1. time, / men / Supreme / long / became / justices / only / Court / a / for

   _____.

2. her / justice / September 25, / began / as / on / work / a / 1981 / she

   _____.

3. Supreme / is / long / becoming / justice / process / a / a / Court

   _____.

4. or / Congress / approve / the / then, / she / decision / asks / he / to

   _____.

5. retired / honor / 2006 / she / in / with

   _____.

E. Listen to the recording and fill in each blank with a suitable word.

TAR3-04
MP3

The United States Supreme Court is the _____ court in the

_____. It was formed over 200 years _____. The United

States has a very _____ law _____ the *US Constitution*.

According to this _____ law, the Supreme Court is _____

up of nine justices, or _____. The justices _____ in

Washington D.C. and do _____ jobs.

The Highest Point

A. Match each word to its definition.

_____ **1.** attempt

a the top of a mountain

_____ **2.** struggle

b to try to do something difficult

_____ **3.** summit

c to try extremely hard to deal with something that causes problems

B. Choose the synonym of the underlined word in the sentence.

1. The exploration was an <u>adventure</u> for the scientists.

a calculation   **b** undertaking   **c** inactivity   **d** boredom

2. As a junior high school student, you are faced with many <u>challenges</u>.

a victory   **b** submission   **c** argument   **d** trial

3. The treatment was <u>successful</u>, and his health got better.

a unfavorable   **b** exhausting   **c** fruitful   **d** barren

C. Fill in the blanks with the right expressions in the box.

considered	necessary	threatened

1. It might be _____ for him to have a small operation.

2. The bank robber _____ to shoot the manager.

3. The principal seriously _____ stepping down.

D. Unscramble the words and write them in the blanks.

1. 8,847 / making / Everest / meters / world's / Mount / high, / it / is / highest / the / mountain

   _____ .

2. 1953, / Everest / unconquered / Mount / stood / until

   _____ .

3. time / were / this / successful / they

   _____ .

4. later, / mountainering / challenged / years / Swiss / successfully / Everest / group / a / three / Mount

   _____ .

5. was / first / to / so / the / do / he / American

   _____ !

E. Listen to the recording and fill in each blank with a suitable word.

TAR3-05
MP3

On May 1, 1963, Jim Whittaker of the United _____ and a fellow _____ from Nepal made an attempt to reach the _____ of Mount Everest. These men _____ to overcome huge _____. Strong winds _____ to blow them _____ the mountain. At great heights it was _____ for them to breathe oxygen from _____. They _____ that one wrong step could _____ them their _____.

A. **Match each word to its definition.**

_____ **1.** dune

(a) to stop something from shaking or falling

_____ **2.** rail

(b) a hill made of sand near an ocean or in a desert

_____ **3.** steady

(c) a bar that is placed around something

B. **Choose the synonym of the underlined word in the sentence.**

1. During the journey, they were able to enjoy the <u>breathtaking</u> scenery.

(a) tedious   (b) monotonous   (c) dreary   (d) thrilling

2. The mayor told us about the <u>events</u> of the past year.

(a) crisis   (b) happening   (c) wealth   (d) misfortune

3. Interestingly, you can gauge the moods of horses by <u>observing</u> their behavior.

(a) rebel   (b) violate   (c) witness   (d) dispute

C. **Fill in the blanks with the right expressions in the box.**

controlled	occasion	soaring

1. We watched the eagle _____ through the air.

2. The toy car is _____ by radio signals.

3. They celebrated the special _____ by having a party.

D. Unscramble the words and write them in the blanks.

1. sure / their / experiment / failure / that / would / they / flying / a / be / were

_____.

2. now-famous / day / windy / winter / cold / was / and / this

_____.

3. facedown, / warmed / lying / the / he / motor / up

_____.

4. alongside / steadying / Wilbur / plane, / the / the / ran / wingtip

_____.

5. slowly / gently, / by / plane / on / then / controlled / the / the / the / pilot, / sand / and / landed

_____.

E. Listen to the recording and fill in each blank with a suitable word.

TAR3-06
MP3

Air _____ was made at Kitty Hawk, North Carolina, on

_____ 17, 1903. Few people were _____ to observe the

_____ event. Those onlookers that were _____ wondered

what the _____ bicycle-makers _____ Dayton, Ohio, were

_____ to now. There were no news _____ _____

to watch this important _____.

A. Match each word to its definition.

_____ **1.** feather

a to jump high

_____ **2.** leap

b to move parts of your body far apart

_____ **3.** spread

c something soft that covers the body of a bird

B. Choose the synonym of the underlined word in the sentence.

1. Thousands of people <u>gathered</u> to watch the fireworks.

a split   **b** disperse   **c** assemble   **d** scatter

2. The two scientists who had studied the property of light reached <u>opposite</u> conclusions.

a positive   **b** identical   **c** synonymous   **d** contrary

3. Frances <u>spends</u> most of her time taking pictures of wild birds.

a replace   **b** expend   **c** preserve   **d** strengthen

C. Fill in the blanks with the right expressions in the box.

covered	efficient	searching

1. The _____ use of time is essential for your success.

2. The police have been _____ for the missing girl for one week.

3. The wall of the classroom was _____ with graffiti.

D. Unscramble the words and write them in the blanks.

1. hold / breath / time / however, / can / for / long / a / their / they

   _____ .

2. penguin's / with / layers / covered / small, / feathers / is / soft / body / of / a / thick

   _____ .

3. penguins / than / feathers / blubber / sometimes / more / and / keep / though / need /
   to / warm, / their

   _____ .

4. as / penguins / together / each / up / 5,000 / as / get / warm / to / other / will / many

   _____ .

5. spread / wings / help / penguins / out / them / their / cool / off / to / these

   _____ .

E. Listen to the recording and fill in each blank with a suitable word.

TAR3-07
MP3

  Unlike _____ birds, penguins cannot fly in the _____ .
Penguins spend almost _____ percent of their time _____ ,
searching for food in the _____ . When they are in the _____ ,
they dive and _____ their wings. It looks _____ they are flying!

  A penguin's body is _____ for the most _____ swimming.
Underwater, penguins can _____ at about 25 kilometers _____
_____ !

First Aid for Snakebites

A. Match each word to its definition.

_____ **1.** mark

a something that connects the brain to other parts of the body

_____ **2.** nerve

b a poisonous American snake that makes a noise when it feels threatened

_____ **3.** rattlesnake

c a small sign of damage, such as a cut

B. Choose the synonym of the underlined word in the sentence.

1. The <u>familiar</u> sound of his voice made her feel relieved.

a timid　　　**b** abnormal　　　**c** usual　　　**d** inattentive

2. They stayed in the <u>nearby</u> city of London for two weeks.

a distant　　　**b** remote　　　**c** separated　　　**d** neighboring

3. There are many things we can do to <u>protect</u> the environment.

a assault　　　**b** defend　　　**c** submit　　　**d** yield

C. Fill in the blanks with the right expressions in the box.

contained	poison	prevent

1. Regular exercise can _____ you from developing heart disease.

2. The wallet _____ many things, such as credit cards and banknotes.

3. The doctor was cruel enough to give _____ to his patients.

D. Unscramble the words and write them in the blanks.

1. rattlesnake / threatened / hikers / feels / nearby / by / a

_____.

2. closer, / raises / head, / attack / get / its / to / and / ready / it / they

_____.

3. this / attack / victim / poisonous / to / the / the / falls / of / ground

_____.

4. been / on / leg / man / bitten / the / the / has

_____.

5. should / tried / aid / do / they / their / first / to / to / snakebite / own / have / on / a / not

_____.

E. Listen to the recording and fill in each blank with a suitable word.

The man's friends get him to a _____. But the man's _____ will never be the _____ again. He has _____ much of its _____. "The problem was not _____ by the snakebite," the doctor _____ the man. It was _____ because his friend cut a _____ in his leg when _____ to draw out the _____. People often _____ the wrong kind of first aid to snakebite _____.

Lights, Camera, Woof!

A. Match each word to its definition.

_____ **1.** collie

_____ **2.** patient

_____ **3.** woof

(a) the sound that a dog makes

(b) a large dog with long hair, used to herd ship

(c) able to stay calm in difficult situations

B. Choose the synonym of the underlined word in the sentence.

1. Not all viruses are <u>dangerous</u> to humans. In fact, some of them are even helpful.

(a) secure   (b) innocent   (c) unsafe   (d) advantageous

2. Surprisingly, the inexperienced actor was given the leading <u>role</u> in the film.

(a) misery   (b) part   (c) hardship   (d) curse

3. It is very cold in June, which is quite <u>unusual</u>.

(a) predictable   (b) typical   (c) plain   (d) extraordinary

C. Fill in the blanks with the right expressions in the box.

envy	noticed	remained

1. Sandra _____ loyal to her best friend throughout the difficult times.

2. Many people _____ Richard his wisdom and courage.

3. I _____ that Mark was nodding his head.

D. Unscramble the words and write them in the blanks.

1. ever / being / imagined / actor / you / an / have

_____?

2. dogs, / their / performing / everyday / these / is / for / work

_____.

3. people / terriers / and / envy / activeness / many / their

_____.

4. notice / dogs / tired / people / their / these / too / when / feel

_____.

5. show, / loyal / Lassie / co-actor, / throughout / remained / Timmy / his / the / to

_____.

E. Listen to the recording and fill in each blank with a suitable word.

TAR3-09
MP3

But performing dogs have _____ special _____. This is

because they sometimes have to do something _____. Therefore,

performing dogs sometimes follow _____ orders. For example,

_____ may order their dogs to _____ through high _____.

In such cases, _____, the trainers do _____ they can to

_____ their performing "_____."

Mail Carriers of the Past

A. Match each word to its definition.

_____ **1.** Colonial

_____ **2.** head

_____ **3.** steal

a someone who is in charge of an organization

b to illegally take something that belongs to another person

c of the original thirteen colonies making up the United States

B. Choose the synonym of the underlined word in the sentence.

1. Using airplanes is still the safest way of <u>carrying</u> people abroad.

a exclude   **b** deliver   **c** surrender   **d** misbehave

2. It was extremely difficult for them to find a <u>reliable</u> source of drinking water.

a inconstant   **b** doubtful   **c** trustworthy   **d** dishonest

3. Queen Elizabeth I <u>ruled</u> England from 1558 to 1603.

a liberate   **b** impress   **c** persuade   **d** control

C. Fill in the blanks with the right expressions in the box.

efforts	horseback	owner

1. In those days, they fought battles primarily on _____.

2. The _____ of the department store was extremely wealthy.

3. Various _____ have been made to bring peace to the community.

D. Unscramble the words and write them in the blanks.

1. time, / Britain / America / long / Great / a / ruled / for

   _____ .

2. America, / letters / easy / Colonial / was / all / sending / at / in / not

   _____ .

3. many / moved / unfortunately, / letters / not / overland

   _____ .

4. result, / owners / carry / other / began / letters / people / ship / for / a / as / to

   _____ .

5. *postriders*, / Post / people, / the / these / Boston / used / Road / called

   _____ .

E. Listen to the recording and fill in each blank with a suitable word.

TAR3-10
MP3

But using the post road to _____ letters was not that _____.

Postriders did not like their jobs very _____, and they often opened

and _____ letters. Sometimes, letters were even _____.

In 1753, Benjamin Franklin became the _____ of the Colonial

_____ system. He made great _____ to make the system

more _____. In _____, Franklin became the first United States

Postmaster _____.

Nantucket Sleighride

A. Match each word to its definition.

_____ **1.** row

a a way in which something can be judged

_____ **2.** sense

b the practice of hunting whales

_____ **3.** whaling

c to cause a boat to move across water by using oars

B. Choose the synonym of the underlined word in the sentence.

1. Contrary to popular belief, you are not likely to be <u>attacked</u> by sharks.

a guard   **b** assault   **c** compliment   **d** shield

2. The doctors used to <u>earn</u> over $70,000 a year.

a restrict   **b** shed   **c** deplete   **d** obtain

3. Keep <u>sharp</u> knives out of the reach of children.

a gentle   **b** inaccurate   **c** pointed   **d** gracious

C. Fill in the blanks with the right expressions in the box.

lasted	protect	thrill

1. It gave the reporter a _____ to finally interview the millionaire.

2. The trial _____ from July 31 to August 30.

3. One of our responsibilities is to _____ endangered species.

D. Unscramble the words and write them in the blanks.

1. ships / boats, / were / whaling / whaling / which / small / had

_____.

2. men / boat / quickly / the / each / rowed / whales / in / five / toward

_____.

3. thing / whales, / would / the / the / the / they / if / water / hit / across / race

_____.

4. sense, / people / dragged / a / the / by / were / in / whales

_____.

5. might / many / depending / ride / hours / kinds / the / the / on / of / for / whales / last

_____.

E. Listen to the recording and fill in each blank with a suitable word.

TAR3-11
MP3

There were many _____ ships _____ Nantucket Island, Massachusetts, in the _____ 1700s. Those ships were _____ to hunt whales. Young _____ knew little about whaling, but many of _____ worked _____ the whaling ships. These lads, who were _____ greenhands, did not _____ much _____. But they got _____ from _____ whales. One _____ those _____ was a "Nantucket sleighride."

Forgotten Inventions

A. **Match each word to its definition.**

_____ **1.** instrument

_____ **2.** wear

_____ **3.** weigh

a to have something on your body

b to have a certain weight

c something that is used for making music

B. **Choose the synonym of the underlined word in the sentence.**

1. Sam <u>attached</u> a small battery to the wristwatch.

a split   b connect   c loosen   d discharge

2. Many houses in the country used to have <u>flat</u> roofs.

a coarse   b rough   c even   d unstable

3. The government struggled to <u>solve</u> the financial crisis.

a disturb   b perplex   c deceive   d answer

C. **Fill in the blanks with the right expressions in the box.**

completely	invention	popular

1. Experts point out that the television is not a great _____.

2. The hotel is extremely _____, thanks to its excellent service.

3. The earthquake _____ destroyed the city in 1865.

D. Unscramble the words and write them in the blanks.

1. people / metal / their / wear / legs / bars / some / on

_____.

2. special / bars / invented / children / 1886, / were / little / metal / in / for

_____.

3. also / toys / metal / could / attach / bars / the / parents / to

_____.

4. result, / were / very / they / quickly / forgotten / a / as

_____.

5. instrument / rod / globes / musical / a / glass / contained / and / this

_____.

E. Listen to the recording and fill in each blank with a suitable word.

TAR3-12
MP3

In 1926, an _____ car was _____ to solve _____ problems.

This _____ car did not _____ as much as other _____ cars.

There was a _____ platform _____ the back of this car. Small

_____ were _____ to the platform. When a _____ wanted to

park his car, he just needed to _____ it to a _____ place. It was

very _____ to move the car to its parking _____!

A. Match each word to its definition.

_____ **1.** colony

a a type of animal that gives milk to its babies

_____ **2.** crop

b a group of animals living together

_____ **3.** mammal

c a plant that farmers grow and sell as food

B. Choose the synonym of the underlined word in the sentence.

1. Pollution has a negative effect on all wild <u>creatures</u>.

a collapse   b animal   c phenomenon   d tragedy

2. Bad habits, such as smoking, can <u>damage</u> your health.

a enrich   b renovate   c perfect   d wound

3. The private school enjoys a good <u>reputation</u>, so many students want to attend it.

a shame   b humility   c fame   d disgrace

C. Fill in the blanks with the right expressions in the box.

care	fear	harm

1. Many children tend to have a _____ of darkness.

2. Unfortunately, too many products do _____ to the environment.

3. People don't _____ for spiders, partly because they look scary.

D. **Unscramble the words and write them in the blanks.**

1. most / play / important / our / animals, / ecosystem / they / in / an / like / but / role

_____ .

2. to / harmful / help / insects / control / bats

_____ .

3. all / live / caves / other / bats / bats / with / not / in / but

_____ .

4. them / by / of / themselves / live / some

_____ .

5. fact, / out / bats / shy / experts / that / are / point / most / in

_____ .

E. **Listen to the recording and fill in each blank with a suitable word.**

TAR3-13
MP3

   Dracula movies have _____ done the most _____ to this _____ creature's reputation. "Thanks to the Count," says one expert _____ to Count Dracula, "_____ people think all bats are _____ vampires."

   Although vampire bats do _____, they only live in the _____, and they are more _____ of animal blood than _____ blood. Other types of bats, which live _____, eat either fruits or _____.

An Island Rises from the Sea

A. Match each word to its definition.

_____ **1.** erupt

a hot liquid rock from a volcano

_____ **2.** lava

b the ground at the bottom of the sea

_____ **3.** seabed

c to send smoke, fire, and rock into the sky in an explosion

B. Choose the synonym of the underlined word in the sentence.

1. Some people believe that comets will <u>destroy</u> the world.

a manufacture　　**b** devastate　　**c** shape　　**d** establish

2. It is <u>helpful</u> to discuss your academic problems with your teacher.

a disadvantageous　**b** unfavorable　　**c** ineffective　　**d** beneficial

3. <u>Surprisingly</u>, not many people know the importance of early education.

a commonly　　**b** normally　　**c** amazingly　　**d** ordinarily

C. Fill in the blanks with the right expressions in the box.

add	appear	origin

1. Unfortunately, small cracks began to _____ in the glass.

2. The cook advised him to _____ more water to the mixture.

3. Many English words, including _huge_ and _hour_, are French in _____ .

D. **Unscramble the words and write them in the blanks.**

1. land / born / volcano / was / thanks / a / to / new

_____.

2. entire / is / off / sometimes, / city / the / an / map / wiped

_____.

3. volcano / sea, / cause / waves / *tsunamis* / erupts / it / called /at / a / giant / can /when

_____.

4. fact, / islands / formed / help / volcanoes / many / are / of / by / in / the

_____.

5. volcano / add / island / maybe / can / Earth / another / an / the / to

_____.

E. **Listen to the recording and fill in each blank with a suitable word.**

For some people, the _____ suddenly seemed to be _____

off the _____ of Iceland. It _____ lava, steam, and rocks

_____ in the air. That _____ because a volcano had

_____ on the seabed 110 meters _____. Surprisingly, an

island — 10 meters _____ and 180 meters _____ — appeared

_____ the water. The year was _____.

Small but Noisy

A. Match each word to its definition.

_____ **1.** carry

_____ **2.** dawn

_____ **3.** sundown

a the time when the sun disappears

b to go a long way

c the time of day when sunlight first appears

B. Choose the synonym of the underlined word in the sentence.

1. Alice was asked to <u>describe</u> the bank robber in detail.

a misbehave   **b** perceive   **c** depict   **d** distort

2. Interestingly, <u>smart</u> students do not always get good grades.

a messy   **b** intelligent   **c** shabby   **d** sloppy

3. Laura is a <u>strong</u> candidate for being class president.

a promising   **b** insecure   **c** fragrant   **d** unsteady

C. Fill in the blanks with the right expressions in the box.

approaching	besides	compared

1. This is a simple job. _____, you can make decent money.

2. Her voice is often _____ to that of an angel.

3. The time is fast _____ when Thomas will leave his hometown.

D. **Unscramble the words and write them in the blanks.**

1. monkey's / carry / kilometers / voice / five / can / to / this / up

_____ .

2. loud / howler / only / kilograms / voice, / weighs / the / its / about / despite / nine

_____ .

3. howlers / sounds / storm / approaching / make / interestingly, / when / is / loud / a

_____ .

4. like / to / places / traveling / howlers / not / distant / do

_____ .

5. not / smart / other / they / monkeys / as / are / as / besides,

_____ .

E. **Listen to the recording and fill in each blank with a suitable word.**

TAR3-15
MP3

Different people _____ the howler's _____ in

different ways. One _____ description _____ its voice

_____ the sounds of jaguars. The jaguars are _____ great

discomfort and making _____ sounds. Another _____

_____ the howler's voice to the _____ of hungry lions.

The Dancing Stallions

A. Match each word to its definition.

_____ **1.** manners

(a) someone who is very good at doing something

_____ **2.** master

(b) the force created when something presses something else

_____ **3.** pressure

(c) polite ways of behaving while you are with other people

B. Choose the synonym of the underlined word in the sentence.

1. In fact, digestion is a highly <u>complex</u> process.

(a) modest   (b) complicated   (c) humble   (d) plain

2. The lung disease usually <u>requires</u> medical treatment.

(a) possess   (b) satisfy   (c) convince   (d) demand

3. The school is very <u>strict</u> about good manners.

(a) mild   (b) tolerant   (c) harsh   (d) inaccurate

C. Fill in the blanks with the right expressions in the box.

methods	strength	skilled

1. The United States tries to attract highly _____ workers to the country.

2. Many teachers were disappointed with traditional _____ of teaching foreign languages.

3. Experts agree that you need more than _____ to win boxing matches.

D. Unscramble the words and write them in the blanks.

1. ever / the / have / *stallion* / heard / you / word

_____?

2. training / school / the / the / strict / is / at / very

_____.

3. Lippizaner / signal / very / horses, / steps / when / stallions / complex / the / they / take

_____.

4. their / riding / usually / horses / using / the / pressure / masters / some / legs, / to / apply / the / by

_____.

5. even / for / special / movements / are / their / there / names

_____.

E. Listen to the recording and fill in each blank with a suitable word.

TAR3-16
MP3

But it is not _____ for the horses to make such dance _____. In fact, they require great _____. Therefore, the riding _____ train the stallions very _____. As a _____, the horses can build strong leg _____. Those muscles help the _____ to make amazing _____.

Under the _____ hands of _____ riders, the proud _____ leap and _____. They seem to be _____ of joy and _____.

Deep-Sea Adventure

A. Match each word to its definition.

_____ **1.** bathyscaphe

_____ **2.** bathysphere

_____ **3.** unexplored

(a) a diving sphere made of steel

(b) not yet explored

(c) a special ship used for deep-sea exploration, which uses gasoline

B. Choose the synonym of the underlined word in the sentence.

1. The citizens are trying very hard to achieve economic <u>development</u>.

(a) basis   (b) progress   (c) decay   (d) downfall

2. These days, many experts question the value of the <u>exploration</u> of space.

(a) illusion   (b) myth   (c) falsehood   (d) investigation

3. Soldiers were sent there for the sole <u>purpose</u> of maintaining peace.

(a) objective   (b) capacity   (c) participation   (d) ability

C. Fill in the blanks with the right expressions in the box.

accurately	succeeded	various

1. At the staff meeting, Michelle raised _____ points about working conditions.

2. At present, we cannot predict the occurrence of an earthquake _____.

3. Amy _____ in losing weight, so she looked slim.

D. Unscramble the words and write them in the blanks.

1. failed / explore / depths / they / ocean / to / but / the

_____.

2. 1930s, / explorers / change / some / that / tried / the / in / to

_____.

3. wanted / deeper / to / Beebe / deeper / ocean / and / into / get / the

_____.

4. 1934, / succeeded / depth / 3,000 feet / Beebe / in / in / over / of / a / reaching

_____.

5. instance, / that / floor / flat / for / know / ocean / not / the / is / we

_____.

E. Listen to the recording and fill in each blank with a suitable word.

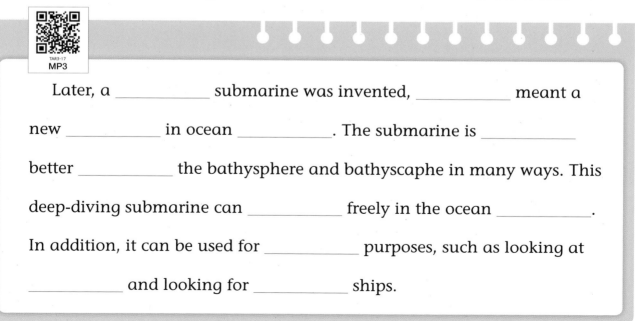

Later, a _____ submarine was invented, _____ meant a

new _____ in ocean _____. The submarine is _____

better _____ the bathysphere and bathyscaphe in many ways. This

deep-diving submarine can _____ freely in the ocean _____.

In addition, it can be used for _____ purposes, such as looking at

_____ and looking for _____ ships.

A. **Match each word to its definition.**

_____ **1.** close

_____ **2.** cocker

_____ **3.** swamp

ⓐ land that is always wet

ⓑ caring about each other

ⓒ a small dog with long ears and silky fur

B. **Choose the synonym of the underlined word in the sentence.**

1. His dog <u>barks</u> every night, which makes it difficult for him to go to sleep.

ⓐ calm ⓑ compose ⓒ growl ⓓ soothe

2. Her mother was greatly <u>relieved</u> to see her again.

ⓐ burdened ⓑ invested ⓒ intensified ⓓ relaxed

3. Natalie was in an <u>unfamiliar</u> place in the dark, so she began to feel scared.

ⓐ imitative ⓑ traditional ⓒ unaccustomed ⓓ conventional

C. **Fill in the blanks with the right expressions in the box.**

dangerously	encourage	lessons

1. Many people have simply failed to learn the _____ of history.

2. Richard drove _____, which led to a traffic accident.

3. Great teachers _____ students to read books extensively.

D. Unscramble the words and write them in the blanks.

1. might / were / boys / think / two / they / you

_____ .

2. happily / Megan's / lived / house / together / they / in

_____ .

3. forest / be / brightly / seemed / shining / to / the

_____ .

4. beauty, / by / forgot / following / Jack / Tom / its / about / fascinated

_____ .

5. Tom's / pleading / Megan / in / the / noticed / eyes

_____ .

E. Listen to the recording and fill in each blank with a suitable word.

Jack looked _____, but Megan tried to _____ him to get _____ of the swamp. But she couldn't think of _____ into the swamp. At that very _____, Tom sprang into the swamp and _____ Jack. Jack could catch Tom's _____ and together they _____ out of the swamp.

Megan felt _____ to know that _____ of her dogs were finally _____. Jack seemed to learn an important _____, and he _____ not fail to follow Tom when going to _____ places.

Mounties, Past and Present

A. **Match each word to its definition.**

_____ **1.** dogsled

a something that people remember

_____ **2.** memory

b a mostly flat area of land in North America, covered in grass

_____ **3.** prairie

c a type of sled pulled by dogs

B. **Choose the synonym of the underlined word in the sentence.**

1. Morocco <u>gained</u> independence from France in 1956.

a wither   b acquire   c contract   d discourage

2. The principal told the English teacher to keep <u>order</u> in his class.

a confusion   b disruption   c proposal   d keeping

3. A new leader was elected, and she would <u>replace</u> her predecessor.

a regret   b revise   c substitute   d terminate

C. **Fill in the blanks with the right expressions in the box.**

recognized	techniques	enforcement

1. As a law _____ professional, Susan knew how to catch criminals.

2. It took a lot of time for his paintings to be _____ as great works of art.

3. Experts point out that more reliable testing _____ should be developed.

D. Unscramble the words and write them in the blanks.

1. chapter / Canadian / began / 1874 / proud / in / in / a / history

    _____ .

2. their / Indians, / Mounties / reliable / dealings / the / the / polite / with / and/ were / in

    _____ .

3. helped / prairie / raging / settlers / also / floods / fight / and / they / fires

    _____ .

4. Canada's / distant / frontier / Mounties / days / memory / now / a / the / of / are

    _____ .

5. uniforms / scarlet / replaced / suits / jackets / and / the / have / brown

    _____ .

E. Listen to the recording and fill in each blank with a suitable word.

TAR3-19
MP3

Their uniforms and crime-fighting _____ may have

_____, but Mountie _____ remain the same. The Mounties

are still _____ for their courage, _____ to

duty, and _____ in law enforcement. In the _____ down

of criminals, today's Mounties _____ with earlier Mounties a

_____ for "always getting their man."

No Strings or Wings

A. **Match each word to its definition.**

_____ **1.** balloon

_____ **2.** hydrogen

_____ **3.** channel

(a) an area of the sea that links two larger areas of water

(b) a large bag made of light cloth, filled with heated gas

(c) a gas that is the lightest element

B. **Choose the synonym of the underlined word in the sentence.**

1. The spaceship was <u>designed</u> to travel over a long period of time.

(a) fade   (b) criticize   (c) punish   (d) plan

2. On August 15, Clinton took a big <u>lead</u> in the the election.

(a) extra   (b) head   (c) handicap   (d) obstacle

3. These public services have been <u>provided</u> effectively and efficiently.

(a) reserve   (b) consume   (c) chase   (d) supply

C. **Fill in the blanks with the right expressions in the box.**

handle	loads	scientific

1. Sometimes, _____ discoveries are made by accident.

2. The inexperienced manager did not know how to _____ the situation.

3. Stronger people are supposed to carry heavier _____.

D. **Unscramble the words and write them in the blanks.**

1. *dirigible* / invented / late / century / during / 19th / was / the / the

_____ .

2. Germany / lead / production / that / the / passenger / took / dirigibles / was / of / in / the / it

_____ .

3. on / US Navy / 1961 / blimps / went / until / late / to / as / as / the / use

_____ .

4. dirigibles / almost / today, / disappeared / but / have

_____ .

5. dirigibles, / kinds / remain / although / other / balloons / use / in / of / not

_____ .

E. **Listen to the recording and fill in each blank with a suitable word.**

TAR3-20
MP3

Balloons have played a _____ role in the story of _____ .

In 1783, a balloon _____ hot air _____ people to fly for

the _____ time. A _____ two years later, a balloon filled

with hydrogen _____ two men _____ the English Channel.

From this time _____, people began to _____ of a day when

balloons would _____ passenger service to _____ places.

MEMO

MEMO

MEMO

TAR3-10
MP3

Think About
Reading ❸